Preaching
from Great
Bible Chapters

Preaching

from Great

Bible Chapters

KYLE M. YATES

Baylor University

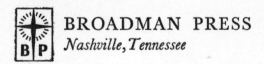

BROADMAN PRESS
Nashville, Tennessee

© 1957 · BROADMAN PRESS

Nashville, Tennessee

All rights reserved.

International copyright secured.

Library of Congress Card Catalog Number: 57–6326

Printed in the United States of America

7.5O56KSP

To

THREE SWEET DAUGHTERS

Jeane Walker Yates

Jean Yates Wooddy

Ellen Yates Tanner

Introduction

By Billy Graham

FROM HAVING KNOWN Dr. Kyle Yates for a number of years, I say without hesitation that he is one of the finest and most thoughtful Christian men I have ever known.

I have carefully read the portion of the manuscript submitted to me for appraisal and have found it doctrinally sound, Christ-centered, and thought-provoking.

Dr. Yates's wide experience and background qualify him for authoritative biblical exegesis and scriptural exposition. In this volume we have a collection of his finest work and effort.

It is a book not only to be read but to be studied. It should not only be used by every minister but perused by every student of the holy Word.

M Y LOVE for preachers has led me to do many things in the hope that these friends might be blessed and their preaching made increasingly effective. The conviction that Bible preaching is the answer to the many problems that confront the churches has deepened through the years. When the people come to know and understand the Word of God, they are ready to commit their lives and their all to the Master. How are they to know unless the Bible is taught and preached? It is my prayer that these studies will inspire and provide material for at least thirteen good expository sermons. It is also hoped that men and women in the churches may find joy and profit in reading these chapters for themselves. Young Christians may discover and become intimately acquainted with thirteen great Bible chapters.

In preparing these studies there has been no effort made to put the material in final form for each minister. The rich, delicious, attractive fruit has been dug up, uncovered, arranged, and put at the immediate disposal of the thoughtful sermon builder. It has been tried and found to be powerful. Congregations have feasted and begged for more.

It will be impossible to give credit where it is due for all the marvelous truths and interpretations that have come out of years of study and preaching on these chapters. My teachers in the seminary and the universities contributed much. The commentaries have all been used over and over again until the richest thoughts of the authors are interwoven into every paragraph. Such mighty men as H. C. Moule, G. Campbell Morgan, W. O. Carver, E. Y. Mullins, Alexander Maclaren, G. G. Findlay, George W. Clarke, John R. Sampey, A. T. Robertson, Guy King, F. W. Farrar, Charles Erdman, A. F. Kirkpatrick, and Franz Delitsch will always remain as great contributors to the store of knowledge I am constantly using. My undying thanks must be given to them.

In quoting from the Bible I have claimed the privilege of using the words of the Authorized Version, the American Standard Version, or words that seem to give a more accurate translation of the original.

Special thanks must be expressed to my beloved wife, to my son, Professor Kyle M. Yates, Jr., and to his wife Jeane, who helped with the manuscript. Without the help of Jewel Butz and Harriet Jones the book would still remain unpublished. They worked diligently and beautifully at the typewriter. Dr. W. R. White of Baylor University and my friends of the Second Baptist Church of Houston, Texas, have been unusually helpful in their unstinted encouragement.

My prayer is that many will be led to know and love these great chapters and that the churches, the homes, and the lives of our land may be strengthened to bring much joy to the heart of our dear Lord and Saviour.

KYLE M. YATES

Waco, Texas

Contents

I. The Amazing Grace

_____*Ephesians II*

HOW DOES ONE dare touch a sublime theological treatise like Paul's precious letter to the Ephesians with the hope that he may make it more meaningful for modern readers? Scores of scholarly men have written, and those glowing pages have been eagerly read by inquiring students of the Word. Hundreds of sermons have been preached on these matchless words. This effort is an additional attempt to interpret them with the hope and prayer that the Holy Spirit may use it to reveal to human minds something of the rich treasures that are ours in this epistle. With it we breathe a fervent prayer that His holy name may be honored and souls may be led to Him for salvation.

INTRODUCTION

In the first chapter Paul thrilled us with the startling announcement concerning the resurrection of our Lord. That great miracle took *power;* it was divine power. The body of our Lord was brought back to full life again. That heavenly power was not used up, nor exhausted, nor turned off. It was kept instantly available for another miracle at any moment. All of it was ready. All of it would be used for each miracle that followed. Paul assures us that this energy would be released to make a new resurrection possible each time a dead soul called out to the Christ for salvation. Simple faith in Him would bring the immediate touch of the Creator's hand.

Paul prayed that we might know in firsthand experience what is God's wondrous hope in calling men for salvation and fellowship, what God expectantly looks for in unspeakable wealth as these new creatures become a part of His treasure, and what power is His to be turned upon any undertaking that looms before Him. Thus Paul prayed concerning God's *hope*, God's *wealth*, and God's *power*. He wanted the Ephesian Christians to see clearly and understand fully these three wonders.

God's measureless power was created for and dedicated to the eternal miracle of working in dead bodies and producing new creatures. That power had been more than sufficient when the body of the Christ lay in the rock-hewn tomb. Not only was Christ miraculously raised from the grave, but He was raised in exaltation to the throne of the Father to sit with Him in majesty and glory. He was made to have absolute authority over every order and form of rule and power and lordship, in this age and in every age that is to come. In addition to all of this transcendent exaltation he was given supreme authority over the church. He was to have the exclusive and complete headship over the entire system of world order or government—including the spiritual direction of all the family of redeemed souls.

Paul uses strong language to picture for us the surpassing greatness of the divine power. He literally heaps up forms of expression to bring out the full force of God's might. In its fulness Christ was lifted bodily from death and the grave, set at the right hand of the Father in glory, and given a supreme place far above all authority and dominion. That place was extended through all the ages of eternity, and Christ reigns triumphantly over the redeemed ones.

What more could be said? Surely Christ has been the recipient of the full power of heaven. No obstacle was big enough to prevail against it. Paul delighted to assure his readers that the full force of all heaven's power was ready to become operative in every trusting soul. The marvelous chapter before us opens to us the golden assurance that God will give us life through Christ. His power will be manifested in that spiritual resurrection. God's miracle is ready for men.

THE SUBLIME EXPERIENCE (1–10)

Before our very eyes we witness the power of God at work in redeeming, transforming, and quickening human souls. Step by step Paul unfolds the divine work. What a miracle is wrought by that power! There is genuine joy as we see the power of God at work and see life flow triumphantly in these new men in Christ Jesus! The same divine power that lifted Christ from among the dead bodies goes out again to take individuals, one by one, to be raised into life and victory. When God's might begins its saving work, souls are made new through divine creation and there is victory. Let us watch the creation of a soul.

Your picture (1–3): Are you ready to watch Paul as he paints your portrait? Do you think you will recognize yourself? Are you willing to let him confront you with the picture that represents you before the miracle was worked? You may be surprised at the portrait. Paul begins by describing the dead material with which God has to work. It is unresponsive, helpless, undesirable—absolutely hopeless. Death is plainly visible as the result of transgressions.

Paul first declares that you once lived and walked and behaved in accordance with the standards of the world about you. You were in step with the pagan world. You were literally one of them, wholly out of sympathy and out of tune with God.

He moves a step further and describes you as fastened to the end of one of the devil's puppet strings, dangling out into space. You were wholly at the will of the evil one, doing his bidding. The ruler of the authority of the air was in full control of your life.

In his third line Paul pictures you as following your natural urges, inclinations, and appetites completely and constantly. The appetites of the natural man determined your behavior. The uninhibited ideas and urges of the natural mind determined your conduct.

Do you recognize your portrait? That is the way you "looked" before the eternal power of God was turned upon you. You were not only going along with a worldly, pagan, sinful crowd but you were under the power of the devil and completely subject to his domination. When he pulled the puppet string you instantly obeyed. In addition to these two pathetic lines in your portrait, the apostle puts in the one that describes you as recklessly abandoned to do and think and say anything and everything that occurred to you as desirable. It might be good, it might be bad, it might be unspeakably immoral, but you followed the urges and desires and lusts of your mind and participated as you liked. How could you ever be like that?

Paul hastened to assure his Gentile readers that they had no monopoly on such behavior. He includes himself and all his Jewish friends in the same picture. Each of them had a personal devil who exerted a strong hold on the behavior and life of every person who was outside Christ. There were no exceptions. There were differences in the depths to which the individual had plunged, but each one stood in pathetic need of the resurrection from death unto life. They could do nothing to bring life. Their friends could not produce life. The power of the devil could not be broken by their own wills or powers or efforts. The devil was unwilling to release his hold upon them. They were doomed! They were helpless! Their cause was hopeless!

In addition to the graphic picture in verses 1–3, Paul paints another brief picture of the Gentiles (verse 12). They were *separate from Christ, alienated* from citizenship in the kingdom of God, *strangers from the covenants of the promise, having no hope, and without God.* Can you imagine anything more heart-rending? How could life be worth living? Nothing in the future held any hope for them. They had no power within themselves to become alive again, to give them hope and abundant life. In Romans 7:24 Paul utters a wail that would fit these unhappy people: "O wretched man that I am! who shall deliver me from the body of this death?" Even as this piercing cry goes up from his soul agony, the power of God is coming to perform the miracle of giving life.

But God (4): The glorious corner has been turned. There is One who can do everything the soul, *dead in trespasses and sins*, needs. God is near, He is able. He is vitally concerned. His great love, His divine mercy, and His plenteous grace make the victory possible. We watch breathlessly as God demonstrates His transcendent power in human lives.

We have been told of Christ's resurrection, His exaltation, His sovereignty, and His headship. We have watched Him, under the impetus of God's mighty power, come forth into a new life as the risen Lord. We see an exhibition of that same miracle-working power bringing life into beings that were hopelessly dead. Love did it! Grace did it! Mercy did it! God did it!

The transformation has begun. The mighty thing has been achieved. The initial stage in salvation has been completed. Notice how Paul, retracing the same steps described for us in 1:20, tells us that the sinner is made to live in Christ Jesus, is raised up and made to sit with Him. (Cf. Galatians 5:17–23, in which Paul describes the terrible fruits that are visible until God comes. After He comes the picture changes to that of a beautiful orchard with nine lovely varieties of choice fruit.) We have been led to look back upon the depths from which we came and forward to the heights to which we travel. He quickened us, raised us, and seated us in the heavenlies.

By grace (5): Fortunately, God was rich in the grace needed for full salvation. He loved with divine love and gave freely of His bountiful supply. Paul emphasizes the fact that salvation is not by works, nor ritual, nor philanthropy, nor character, but by the amazing grace of God. The victory is full and complete. The shackles of death have been removed. The chains of the devil have been broken. The appetites and desires have been changed. Life has taken the place of death. All this is the gift of the eternal One who loves, who has mercy, and who has grace.

Through faith (trust) (8): We may have a small part in the great transaction. How may we enter into the plan and contribute our bit? What is faith? Perhaps the best word to use for this context is "trust." The one who is to be saved must throw himself wholly upon the Lord in simple child-like trust. Salvation is not merely a thing of the head, but it is very definitely a thing of the heart and a thing of the hand. We must receive Him. Our trembling hands must go into His hand. Jesus said: "As many as received him, to them he gave power to become the sons of God, even to them that believe on his name" (John 1:12). Grace is God's part. Faith is ours. Salvation is wholly the miraculous work of God, but the link that makes it operative in us is the simple trust we put in our Lord and Saviour. His atoning death has made our salvation possible. His grace brings it to us. Our faith in Christ makes it ours. Paul says clearly that no other plan of salvation can ever be available. This is God's one and only way. It is an adequate way and an eternal way.

Trophies of grace (7): In verse seven we are introduced to one of God's choice secrets. He has a great longing in His heart to see His redeemed ones make such progress in growth and purity and winsomeness that He can exhibit them one day as His prize trophies of grace. His gift of His only begotten Son to die on Calvary to make atonement for the sins of the world was His biggest investment. Salvation was purchased. Atonement was completed. Those who accept Him are instantly born again. God will receive His highest joys in seeing these ransomed ones become rich in the qualities that befit Christians. One day he will proudly exhibit them as new creatures in Christ Jesus who have become like Him. Out of material so unlikely, so useless, and so unattractive He has fashioned new creatures through whom He might show the riches of His grace.

Are you getting ready for God's great exhibition of choice trophies? Are you one of them? Can He be proud of you? Do your thoughts, your words, your deeds please Him? Are you showing forth the spirit that will be chosen as His finest product of redeeming grace? He has given His only begotten Son to die for you. He is depending on you. He looks to that high hour when demonstration shall reveal true champions. It will delight His heart to see you grow beautiful in the Christian graces.

God's poems (10): In verse ten Paul uses a word (*poiema*) to describe this newly created individual. Through faith in Christ the believer has felt the creating touch of God's miraculous power. He stands fresh and quivering before his Creator. Paul declares that he is "God's poem." The old verb *poieo* means to work or fashion. The Greek ending gives the idea of result. The old translation "his workmanship" is correct but rather colorless, for the Greek word carries with it the idea of a beautiful hand-tooled masterpiece. The word "poem," a transliteration of *poiema*, is an accurate translation of the word. Paul is saying, "You are God's harmonious, beautiful, exquisite, lovely creation—His poem." God is the Creator. When He fashions something, it is perfect. The poem is the perfect and beautiful creation!

The tree is not a poem. It is a lovely prose piece. The horse, in all of its beauty, is not a poem. The most beautiful orchid in the world is not a poem. The mountain in its majestic grandeur is not a poem. Not even the most perfect baby can be classed as a poem. He is a special creation of the Creator and is precious to all of us, but he does not qualify as Paul uses this word. The apostle reserves this word for the redeemed child of God, one who has found himself in sin and slavery to the devil, has looked to Jesus in simple faith, and has found the miracle of the resurrection operative in him. He is a new creature in Christ. He is God's poem. It is a genuine joy to know that we are such rare creations and to understand God's estimate of us. We must be even more careful in our conduct now that we have learned that we are God's poems.

These special poems are created in Christ Jesus. The divine blueprint is followed. The breath of God is breathed into them to fit them to bring forth good works. Paul makes it clear that the works in no sense procure salvation, but that they unceasingly flow from salvation. These works are unmistakable evidences of salvation. They are fruits that come as God's choice treasures. He planned them for His own glory. He reaps His choice dividends as saved souls produce good works. How rich life becomes as we sense something of God's love for us, His plans for our lives, His infinite patience in making us His poems, His purposes for us, and His joy in seeing evidences of good works for the days ahead.

GOD'S ULTIMATE PURPOSE (11–22)

The plan of God goes beyond the moment of regeneration. Redeemed souls are not to be left in lonely isolation but are to be wrought carefully into the family of God and are destined to become vital parts in the building of God's holy church. He has a place for Gentiles in His church. Each of them is duty bound to assume his responsibilities and become basic parts in the structure. Jew and Gentile become fellow Christians in this new fellowship. The eternal purpose of God is gradually and beautifully worked out in both.

Then . . . now (11, 13): The amazing change that had come about in the Gentiles was a matter of unending delight to Paul. He reminded them of their former state. They were "outside" everything that was spiritual and eternal. They could claim none of the covenants and rights and promises of Israel. They were not members of God's chosen people. They were completely separated from Christ. They could claim no part in the sacred heritage reserved especially for God's people. As a result, they had no hope and no God. Many gods were theirs, but not God. Many passing hopes were theirs, but no real hope. How poor can a man be?

But now in Christ Jesus ye that once were far off are made nigh in the blood of Christ (13). What a wonderful change the blood of Christ has made! Paul sees that Christ's death was the one triumphant victory that made other victories possible. It procured redemption for every individual on earth. Jesus is the Saviour of the Gentiles as perfectly as He has become the fulfilment of all Jewish hopes. In his atoning death He brought all men to His side for salvation. That salvation was made effective through simple trust in Him.

Jew and Gentile together in one sacred relationship in Christ formed the re-created material out of which God was constructing His church. All walls and fences and barriers and veils were broken down and removed by the Son of God, who became the world's blessed Redeemer. It was God's grace that made these things possible. Because of Jesus' vicarious sacrifice, Jew and Greek can come together to the throne of grace knowing that ample provision has been made for both and that each is welcome. In coming close to Him they find themselves brought close together. No dividing lines to create bitterness and suspicion are allowed in the church purchased by His blood.

Our peace (14): Paul hastened to assure the Ephesians that these precious possessions were theirs because *He is our peace.* Isaiah had called the Messiah the "Prince of peace." The Lord Jesus Christ died to create peace. No person is left out. No one is beyond the reach of the peace He provides. The old architectural arrangement that made it unlawful and impossible for Gentiles to enter the temple area was but a reminder of a similar barrier that kept outsiders from the divine supply of grace. God had intended that all men should be one, with free and full access to every area of His grace. Men had created barriers and hostilities and enmities. Christ came to abolish such unchristian things.

"When He poured out His blood on Calvary He destroyed both walls—the one that separated men from one another (Jew and Gentile) and the one that separated men from God."

In His atoning death, Christ made peace possible. No longer need hostility and estrangement and separation have place in God's beautiful creation. A new day had dawned. Peace could reign. The peace of God was available for all men. All the members of the Trinity combined to reconcile man to God. What a treasure these Gentiles could enjoy since they could think of God as *Father!* All the warmth and tenderness and love of a Heavenly Father could now be theirs. Here is indeed a contrast to verses 1, 2, 3, and 12. In addition to the joy of having the Father as their very own, they were to be surrounded, animated, led, inspired, and penetrated by the Spirit. In finding Christ as Saviour they had found the Father and the Spirit as constant possessions. Their days were to be filled with all that the heart could desire.

Now therefore (19): The grandeur of their privileges in grace is stressed in order that these Gentiles might recognize God's purpose in this reconciling and unifying work. Privilege involves and implies responsibility. The miraculous work on new material of unregenerate humanity has guaranteed a fresh new start for them. Not only do they have high privileges in Christ but they need to consider that God continues to work out His eternal purpose in them and that each Christian has a specific position in accomplishing that purpose. The miracle God worked to effect salvation was wholly His effort. The continuance of His work of grace in the world is definitely to include their participation to the fullest measure.

Paul encouraged them to realize their new status. They

were *no longer strangers* and visitors among the people of God's realm, *but rather fellow citizens of the saints and even members of God's household*. They were fully and completely "at home" in the Father's house. No room was closed to them, no privilege denied them. They were in good standing. They belonged. They were "heirs of God and joint-heirs with the Lord Jesus Christ." In the church all were even in their privileges, their possessions, and their responsibilities. The ground is level at the cross. The saints are designated as the *family*, a *building*, and a *body*. Each member has his possessions and privileges together with the rest.

Having been built (20): Paul makes it clear that the divine Architect is building a glorious building according to His own design and plan. He assures his readers that each of them is actually built into this structure. They are selected individually to be an integral part of His completed house. If we look back for a moment we will be slightly surprised that such unlikely, undesirable, unpromising material as we found pictured in verses 1, 2, 3, and 12 should be chosen for the choicest of all God's projects.

The structure is described as one that "groweth unto a holy temple in the Lord." Daily it becomes more like Him who is holy. It grows as new miracles bring new members into the family. Each one presents a new personality, a new opportunity, and a new problem. Each comes into possession of divinely bestowed dignity and treasures and is expected to fit into the place provided for him in the specifications for the building. The growth is to be *in the Lord*.

The foundation of any building is exceedingly important. This fact becomes increasingly true when we consider such a building as Christ's holy perfect building. Paul assures his readers that the doctrines stressed by Old Testament prophets and by New Testament prophets and apostles are the foundation stones used to give security and stability to the structure. This eternal building (His church) is built on the foundation that the apostles and prophets have laid. The solid foundation which these men of God built is the enduring basis for truth and doctrine in all the ages. They were men called, endowed, and taught to reveal God's will for men and to interpret His actions in the light of His whole purpose and program.

In his first letter to the Corinthians, Paul wrote, "According to the grace of God which was given unto me . . . I laid a foundation, and another builds thereon. But let each man take heed how he build thereupon. For other foundation can no man lay than that is laid, which is Jesus Christ" (3:10–11). In Ephesians 2:20 he adds, "Jesus Christ himself being the chief corner stone." Christ is the stone at the angle of the structure by which the architect takes the bearings of the walls throughout the entire building. He makes the security and balance and perfection of the building possible.

The foundation of a building is supremely important. The Empire State Building in New York City is tall, stately and magnificent. It towers into the air for more than twelve hundred feet (102 stories). Such a skyscraper needs a strong and dependable foundation. We are told that forty-six feet below the level of the street is a solid rock into which is anchored steel cables, reaching over more than two acres of that remarkable rock. The building is literally tied on with steel ropes to the rock. No one need worry about the strength and security of that mighty tower after he has examined the foundation. Surely it is founded upon a rock. The Christian has no need for fear as he becomes aware of the eternal foundation stone he has in Christ Jesus. He is our cornerstone. He is an anchor sure and steadfast. He is our Rock of ages. No other foundation can be found to bring salvation to a soul.

Fitly framed together (21): God seeks to build a holy sanctuary. He recognizes individual participation as a necessity. Whether we render the Greek phrase "each several building" or "all the building," we see the divine Architect calling on every available unit to become a vital part in the perfect structure He has envisioned. He sees one great building coming gradually to completion under His eyes and rising to the last inch of perfection in fulfilment of His dream. Each individual must take account of the full meaning of his membership in the family of God. These Gentiles have been brought into the family, and each one is singled out as a chosen and honored unit in the completion of the masterpiece. The gospel has reached out into all races and peoples. No one of these is to be left out of His plans. Each is equally important, equally privileged, and equally obligated.

As the building grows in compactness and solidarity, the idea is that each member shall major on precision work. No slight, no short cut, no failure, and no shoddy material can be countenanced. Every detail must be wrought out carefully, faithfully, and beautifully. When the eye of the Architect looks upon it, He must be pleased. Absolute perfection is demanded.

It is not enough, however, to have multitudes of small examples of perfection without regard for the proper fitting into the other parts and into the harmonious whole. Each person works with diligence and care and skill to see to it that his part of the building fits perfectly in completing God's plan. Progressive, co-operative, thoughtful work is described. There is actual growth, symmetry, and coherence; there is daily progress in perfection of design.

In a West Texas encampment ground is an auditorium built to seat more than two thousand people. Not a single post or column is visible within the structure, and no beam of any kind ties it together. The roof is the secret. It is called a lamella roof. It is made up of thousands of short lamellas, each cut from ordinary pine lumber. They vary in length from thirty inches to seven feet. In the entire roof no piece of timber is longer. Each one of these little lamellas is bolted in three places to the adjacent lamellas all the way over and across the entire roof. Beginning at one corner and going completely over all the wide space, the roof grew by the complete incorporation of these small units, one by one, until the roof was completed. It is a perfect illustration of our text. Snows and winds and rains have no power over this perfect work.

The Holy Spirit makes such growth possible. He understands the blueprint and the specifications. He knows the way perfectly. He knows and understands the other individuals about us. He knows and interprets the Word of God to our minds so that symmetrical and harmonious growth is possible. He brings the encouragement and challenge that make full victories possible. He seeks our commitment, our willingness, our efforts, our continual listening to His voice of direction, and our enthusiastic, joyous participation in making God's dream come true. We are to remember that all of this is for the glory of God. It is for Him that we spend all our days in the building of that wondrous sanctuary. It is a cathedral —not yet finished—where the Presence can find His happiest enjoyment and fullest satisfaction.

It is through this sanctuary that men are to see the full manifestation of the grace of God. It is to be the medium through which He may interpret the plenteous grace that He has provided for men and women of all races, lands, and ages. That church He has been building. The material was unlikely, unbecoming, unholy, and undesirable, but out of it He has continued to build this holy sanctuary. He loved us, quickened us, raised us, seated us with the saints, and now rejoices as He sees His church growing daily into the fulfilment of His dreams. We can now see more clearly the meaning of verse seven: *That in the ages to come he might shew the exceeding riches of his grace in his kindness to us through Christ Jesus.*

How He must rejoice in anticipation as He prepares trophies of grace for the full manifestation! The church is an unveiling of God in His redeeming grace. His full changing of dead, vile, hostile, unsightly creatures into instruments of beauty and glory will show forth the perfection of His grace. His church is the sanctuary where He can dwell in eternal enjoyment of such victories.

Bishop Moule summarizes the chapter in these beautiful words: "Thus closes the special revelation of the plan and nature of the great Living Sanctuary, built on the Son, by the Spirit, for the Father, to be the scene of the manifestation of His Glory to whatsoever spectators Eternity shall bring to see it." [1]

In this holy building there is a place for everybody—small stones, big stones, square stones and round stones, irregular stones and orthodox stones. In this divinely inspired fellowship the Holy Spirit seeks to lead us to plant ourselves in the fullest perfection of His holy habitation. "For ye are the temple of the living God" (2 Cor. 6:16). He makes possible a life of power, a life of fullest participation and richest satisfaction.

---

[1] *Epistle to the Ephesians (Cambridge Bible for Schools and Colleges,* ed. J. J. S. Perowne [Cambridge: The University Press, 1889]).

Breathe, O breathe Thy loving Spirit
Into every troubled breast!
Let us all in Thee inherit,
Let us find the promised rest;
Take away our bent to sinning;
Alpha and Omega be;
End of faith, as its beginning,
Set our hearts at liberty.

Finish, then, Thy new creation;
Pure and spotless let us be;
Let us see Thy great salvation
Perfectly restored in Thee:
Changed from glory into glory,
Till in heaven we take our place,
Till we cast our crowns before Thee,
Lost in wonder, love, and praise.

CHARLES WESLEY

Psalm XXIII

The Lord is my shepherd; I shall not want. He maketh me to lie down in green pastures: he leadeth me beside the still waters. He restoreth my soul: he leadeth me in the paths of righteousness for his name's sake. Yea, though I walk through the valley of the shadow of death, I will fear no evil: for thou art with me; thy rod and thy staff they comfort me. Thou preparest a table before me in the presence of mine enemies: thou anointest my head with oil; my cup runneth over. Surely goodness and mercy shall follow me all the days of my life: and I will dwell in the house of the Lord for ever.

II. The Good Shepherd

WHAT A PRECIOUS message to needy souls! How refreshing! How comforting! Men and women and boys and girls of all countries, races, and ages have found in these simple verses a charm, a winsomeness, a fragrance, and a full sweetness that lift and hearten and bless. Surely we have in them the pearl of the Psalms, David's prime jewel, the refreshing oasis in life's desert, the holy place of God's sublime revelation to His children. In these familiar words we find the voice of a human soul securely nestling in the arms of a loving God.

We recognize, too, that the Holy Spirit speaks to all of us through this unbelievably fresh statement of childlike trust. It reaches the depths of our hearts, inspiring drooping spirits and encouraging every heart. It brings comfort like a breath from above. It pulls aside the curtain and reveals to us the picture of God Himself as the One who does all that can be desired for each of His own. It has charmed away griefs, driven out doubts, comforted sorrowing ones, poured the genuine balm of consolation where it was most needed, and given miraculous power for action leading on to victory. Courage has come; confidence has returned; consolation has replaced mourning and heart distress; joy bells have been awakened in hearts that needed heavenly music: these words have been doing all this for three thousand years. They promise to keep on singing through the generations of time until our dear Lord shall return for His own.

This little poem lies between the psalm of the cross and the psalm of the crown. In Psalm 22 there is pictured the Good Shepherd who died, the Saviour who suffered (cf. John 10). In Psalm 24 we see the chief Shepherd reappearing in glory, bringing crowns (cf. 1 Pet. 5:4). In the twenty-third Psalm our Lord is presented as the living Shepherd, keeping His redeemed ones all through life's difficult journey (cf. Heb. 13:20–21). The shepherd psalm will mean more to us as we view it in this setting. Strength and steadiness and serenity and security will be ours as the message of this psalm breaks in upon us.

David wrote it. It was almost certainly the contribution of his more mature years. He had suffered deeply and had tasted the bitter cup. He had known the trying path, the tragic need, the heart-rending hurt, the blessed comfort, the wise guidance, the ever-present touch of the Shepherd's hand, and the satisfaction of having safely come through many testings. David knew the Shepherd; he had found Him everlastingly adequate. He rejoiced to give his testimony to the millions who would need to know the great Shepherd. Thirty centuries have passed since his day. All the buildings, equipment, and relics of that hour have passed away except this beautiful treasure, which remains as a lullaby for children and a challenging inspiration for all ages.

The psalm is strangely personal, unusually descriptive of the man David. As we study it we learn several things about him. He knows that he is a needy creature. Full confession is made of his utter dependence, his proneness to go astray, and his ignorance. He felt keenly his pitiful helplessness, his utter lack of ability to protect himself, his longing for companionship, and his hopes for an eternal home at the end of the journey. He makes it clear that he is speaking from ripe experience. He has tried the keeping power of God and has found that in every area of life the Lord has proved to be the loving Shepherd described in these verses. In all of life's experiences David found Him faithful.

The psalmist reveals his great love for his Shepherd. A grateful love is evident in every line. David had fallen in love with his divine Guide, and every moment with Him was a distinct joy. That sweet fellowship has given him a sense of the eternal security of one who trusts and leans on the Shepherd. A beautiful assurance runs through the psalm transforming it into a shout of triumph. No emergency can be too much for him. No dark valley can be a conqueror. No hour in all of life can be without victory, for the eternal Shepherd guarantees it. David delights to claim the Shepherd as his own. How he does like to use the word "my!" We too can appropriate the Shepherd through faith.

JEHOVAH IS MY SHEPHERD

Imagine a poet's telling us that God is a shepherd. The word "Jehovah," often translated "the Lord," is the personal name for our Father God, the God and Father of our Lord Jesus Christ. He is the eternal One. He is the living One, the self-existent Being, the eternal I Am. He is unchangeably the same. He created all things. He is, always has been, and always will be. The Hebrew word *Yhwh* could not be pronounced except by the high priest in the holy of holies on the Day of Atonement. In order to make it usable for all the people, the vowels from the word "Lord" were attached to the sacred consonants. In English translation the word thus formed is "Jehovah." The actual word was probably *Yahweh*.

The psalmist dares call the eternal God his shepherd. A thousand years later Jesus took up David's beautiful identification of God as Shepherd by declaring, "I am the good shepherd." Jesus' use of "I am" here suggests God's use of "I am" in Exodus 3:14–15 as a name for Himself. In thus using "I am," Jesus identified Himself with Jehovah, combining a high and exalted word for the eternal God and the tender word for a loving Saviour. Thus we find coupled the concept of power with that of sympathy, love, and tenderness. He is sovereign Lord over all and at the same time a loving friend and intercessor and Saviour.

The word "shepherd" originally meant "friend," "guide," "companion." The meaning was so apparent in the manner and character of the shepherd that the word came into common use. The psalmist is saying, "God is that to me—kind, loving, solicitous, and devoted." The shepherd was also equipped to protect and guide his beloved sheep. The Lord's hands, His eyes, His heart, His faithfulness, His strength, his matchless tenderness, and His undying love for His sheep make Him the ideal Shepherd. When we turn to the New Testament for Jesus' own appraisal of Himself, we see how perfectly He was the Good Shepherd. In every way imaginable He measured up to the deeper meaning of that figure. In no point is there the slightest lack. David caught a sublime truth and put into writing a New Testament theme too significant for words.

The little word "my" is the transforming word. What a profound difference it makes! The psalmist did not speak theoretically or generally. He knew the Shepherd as "my"

Shepherd. Appropriation by personal faith makes Him mine. Only as He comes to be *my Shepherd* can I know the full meaning of a relationship like the one described in this psalm.

I SHALL NOT WANT

No one in the world can say, "I shall not want," except as he can claim the Lord Jesus as Shepherd-Saviour. The man of the world can but cry out, "I perish here with hunger." Listen to Paul as he shouts, "My God shall supply all your need according to his riches in glory by Christ Jesus" (Phil. 4:19). In another place the psalmist says, "The young lions do lack, and suffer hunger: but they that seek the Lord shall not want any good thing" (34:10). In these words—"I shall not want"—no reference is made to a future tense. What David really says is, "I never want for anything." At no time in all of life, here or in eternity, can there be a lack of anything needful for carrying out God's will.

How rich we are! So rich we are that every need will be supplied, moment by moment, from the Lord's vast treasure house. The answer is never late. It is a part of His plan to know and anticipate our every need. How can one be so rich? No multimillionaire could ever qualify because of mere earthly wealth. No bountiful provision such as this could be imagined except as we imagine the gifts of our Shepherd. How this knowledge should thrill us! How it should humble us! How it must challenge us! *I shall not want.*

My Shepherd is as strong and powerful and able as He is gentle and kind and good. Power is coupled with gentleness, strength with tenderness, authority with grace, and love with holiness. He is able to save from cruel foes, from deep chasms, from assaults of the tempter, from sin's power; He can keep in the hour of sorrow or the experience of death. All of life is under His control. No moment is beyond His divine reach.

In Palestine the hills were bare and rocky and hot. The patches of good grass were scarce. The oases were not easily available. The good shepherd knew where to find them, understood the need for them, and worked diligently to get his sheep off the hot, rocky hillsides into a quiet place where rest and refreshment might be found. How welcome were these secluded spots! David knew how necessary they were in the lives of his sheep. In order to get the rest they needed, the sheep must have a feeling of security, they must have plenty of nourishing food and water, and they must be willing followers of the shepherd.

The psalmist recognized the hand of the great Shepherd in his own life. How tenderly he had been led into the kind of soul rest that had given him the needed nourishment and refreshment for the rough going. He knew the kind of security that made him serene and quiet within. He knew the soul-filling joy of good spiritual food. He remembered the often-repeated drinks of cool, refreshing water from the Shepherd's exhaustless supply. How life had been changed and blessed all the way by the streams of grace flowing daily into his rough life! The verb *"nahal,"* which he uses, is a beautiful pastoral word meaning "to lead gently" or "peacefully."

Our Good Shepherd said, "He that cometh to me shall never hunger; and he that believeth on me shall never thirst" (John 6:35). "My sheep shall never perish, neither shall any man pluck them out of my hand" (John 10:28). We are wondrously cared for by One who delights to provide the needs of those who have trusted themselves to the Shepherd. Remember His precious words to his faithful apostle, "My

grace is sufficient for thee" (2 Cor. 12:9). The one who has
the hardest road to travel can be assured of the Shepherd's
tender thoughtfulness, which guarantees every needed blessing all life through. Life makes heavy demands. How can
anyone blunder along the difficult journey without the personal touch of the Shepherd's hand? When hunger for spiritual food gnaws unceasingly, how can he go on? In vain
does he seek to appease the hunger with the husks the swine
eat. Our Good Shepherd calls out to him, "Come unto
me, all ye that labor and are heavy laden, and I will give
you rest" (Matt. 11:28).

HE RESTORETH MY SOUL

Can you detect the sob in David's soul as he pulls the curtain aside and reveals the darkest moment in his life? Read
again Psalms 51 and 32, and sense something of the poign-
ant suffering experienced by the sinner as he looked at his
soul and found it in such pathetic condition. How could he
ever come back to his former place of usefulness? How could
he expect his damaged soul to function again? What magic
remedy could cleanse and renew a warped, diseased, sinful
heart? How could an infected blood stream be made clean
and pure again? It is beautiful to see the way he went about
begging forgiveness, step by step, and even more beautiful
to hear him tell us (Psalm 32) of the victory he experienced
as the limitless grace of his loving Shepherd brought forgiveness and cleansing and a new heart. The joy bells rang again.
In this precious line he declares, *He restoreth my soul*. Note
especially the little word "my."

As precious as that experience is we may be sure that
David meant to include far more in his statement. It is the
habit of the Shepherd to *restore* the soul. No matter what
has happened or what the condition of the soul is, He is

able and willing to bring about full restoration. No case is too hard for Him.

The word "restore" would naturally include the bringing back of one who had strayed from his rightful place or his rightful owner as well as one who had lost his vigor, health, and purity. The story of the shepherd who went into the hills to seek and find and bring back the straying sheep is one of the best illustrations of the Good Shepherd's love. The song "The Ninety and Nine" will always move our hearts. The Good Shepherd can never be satisfied as long as even one of His sheep is straying in the ways of sin. *He restoreth my soul.*

Simon Peter could give us a firsthand account of the Shepherd's seeking and restoring. Although Jesus had warned him that temptation would come and had prayed that he would not yield, Peter had denied his Lord. Then Jesus met Peter alone on that memorable Sunday afternoon. Jesus won Peter back before the early morning breakfast by the sea, empowering him to go forth as a beloved missionary to others. Surely the same Shepherd can and will do as much for each one of us. How we need the touch of His holy hand to restore the music of our souls, the ringing of joy bells, the lost radiance, the clear testimony, the vibrant voice, the powerful witness, and the wondrous Christian influence He would have us exhibit all the days of our lives. Why blunder along through life, weak or frail or sinful or powerless, when the Good Shepherd makes it His business to *restore* the soul? Maybe your soul needs restoration as much as David's did. Life is rapidly running out. It may be later than you think!

HE LEADETH ME

This word for "lead" is *nihah* and means to guide, direct, or lead carefully toward a definite goal according to a definite plan or blueprint. It is a strong word. The shepherd knew that it was necessary to have the sheep take a certain course and arrive at the chosen place. He took over and guided according to the plan, using whatever force was needed to direct the sheep in the appointed way.

The same sheep that was gently led to the oasis for rest and shade and refreshment now finds himself guided out into the struggle of the way again. He cannot hope to loll about the still waters, the soothing shade, and the quiet place of rest all the time. The stern test of the open road with its steep climbs, hot rocks, bare hillsides, uninviting landscapes, and dangerous turns must be endured. It is here that the shepherd reveals a different side of his character. He has a definite plan. His will must be carried out.

David understood fully that our lives are not to be spent entirely in rest, soft living, and sheltered moments. Life is a serious matter. Life is a struggle. We are put here for a purpose. Stern discipline must follow rest. The Shepherd must direct our energies and guide our steps into the going that may be rougher than we had expected. Refreshment must be followed by strenuous effort. Our Lord says that the Good Shepherd "goeth before them, and the sheep follow him" (John 10:4). His way may lead over the stony mountain track or through ugly surroundings for days of weary plodding, but we may be sure that He always guides through right or straight paths. His way is always consistent with divine rectitude. "He knoweth our frame: he remembereth that we are dust" (Psalm 103:14). We may rest assured that His way is right even though we may not understand it all until the tapestry is completed and we can see the other side where the divine pattern is worked out.

David was far enough along the road to be able to see something of God's finished work and to understand some things that had seemed mysterious to him. Someday you will see and understand and know that His way of leading was best for you and for His mosaic. We may rejoice to recall that our Shepherd is already pledged to lead us *for his name's sake*. Because of His name and His honor He will bring us safely into the fold. The challenge to us is to walk very close to our Shepherd, even when the following is hard, knowing full well that He knows the way and will bring us to the fullest realization of that which fits His plan. "Where He leads me I will follow."

I WILL FEAR NO EVIL

We have found that the shepherd led to quiet waters for rest and refreshment and then guided his sheep out into straight paths of struggle and stern testing. We also know that once in awhile it became necessary to lead through dangerous mountain defiles where darkness, steep cliffs, and sudden bends in the road made the going exceedingly hazardous. Cruel men and hungry beasts might lurk in hidden places to exact their toll from the flock. It was not a pleasant journey. Fear, panic, pain, and even death might await the sheep in this perilous adventure. They could not make their way alone, but with a powerful, courageous shepherd they could make the hazardous journey in safety. David could remember many times when he had dared to lead his sheep through these gorges in order to get them to a place of safety and plenty on the other side. He was happy in the thought that his skill and devotion as a shepherd had given the victory on all these occasions. He was keenly aware of the tragic experiences that came to some of his flock when wilful disobedience had brought destruction.

How delighted he is to record his debt of gratitude to his divine Shepherd, who had made dangerous places safe by

His sacrificial leading! In all the narrow paths beside precipices filled with danger he had known the grip of the Shepherd's hand on his. He had been free from fear because of the presence of the One who gave victory.

The word *ge*—translated "valley"—indicates a narrow, treacherous defile or gorge. It might have a path through it. It might have steep cliffs on one side or on both. The word *tsalmaweth* can be translated "shadow of death" or "deep darkness." This is its first appearance in the Bible. It can include the experience of death, but note that it here means "shadow." The psalmist is not confining his thought to death, but rather seeks to describe any serious trying or testing time in life. Some of these experiences are darker, more desperate, and more excruciating than the moment we call death. The psalmist clearly pictures a heart-rending moment when danger, temptation, pain, anguish, or some tragic occurrence almost overwhelms one. How can one stand up under these terrible times of testing? How can one who is not in the keeping of the Shepherd hope to make his way through this deadly defile? How can he defend himself against the tempter, endure the pain, or live through the sorrow? The answer is that the Shepherd makes the difference.

David declares that he had passed through these pathetic moments of testing without fear. His support was the assurance of the Shepherd's presence: *for thou art with me.* The psalmist was speaking from experience. He had passed through these trying times. He knew beyond words that his Shepherd had been at his very finger tips. The darkness, the danger, the beasts, the robbers, and the unseen pits of destruction had all been powerless to harm him, for he was led by his Shepherd.

Such trying times test the quality of the soul. Weak places are revealed. We learn how frail we are, how utterly inadequate we are. We look up and discover the storm when it is darkest about us. We reach out for the Shepherd and for His golden words of comfort, encouragement, and direction. We lean on Him and fall in love with Him in the night of danger and suffering. In life, in death, in eternity David was aware of the certainty of the Shepherd's presence. Yes, the hour of death is definitely included in this picture. For the Christian that experience should not be dark, for the Shepherd is near. We realize that the dark valley leads but to the sunlit hills on the other side and that the theme song of the Christian could well be "Sunrise Tomorrow."

In an ancient city there is a long, dark, narrow tunnel leading down into the ground. When one dares to go all the way through the darkness, he emerges at the entrance of a beautiful oriental palace, brilliant with lovely colors in the sunlight. With our Guide we make our way without fear *through the valley of the shadow* into the glory land beyond.

THEY COMFORT ME

All through God's Word we find the beautiful word *naham,* which is translated "comfort." Isaiah brought us the lovely line, "Comfort ye, comfort ye my people, saith your God" (40:1). Our loving Father has always wanted to bring comfort to needy hearts. The work of the Holy Spirit is to bring comfort. Paul, in his second letter to the church at Corinth, says: "Blessed be God, even the Father of our Lord Jesus Christ, the Father of mercies, and the God of all comfort; who comforteth us in all our tribulation, that we may be able to comfort them which are in any trouble, by the comfort wherewith we ourselves are comforted of God" (1:3-4).

We are constantly in need of the comfort which God gives. It is the divine touch that helps one who is choked with grief or fear to breathe freely. Those who are making their way along the dark mountain gorge of the shadow need an extra portion of that breath from heaven. To know that the Good Shepherd is near is a great comfort.

David declares that the *rod* and the *staff* comfort him. The *rod* was the special club or weapon of defense the shepherd carried to give him extra power over foes. He needed to be well-armed against wild beasts and wicked men who would rob him of his flock. The *staff*, or crook, was used by the shepherd almost constantly to keep his own sheep in line, to count them as they came into the fold, to extricate them from ravines or holes, and to chastise them when such treatment was needed. How could these two instruments be expected to bring comfort? David recognized these two man-made tools as aids to carrying into effect the powerful protecting power of the shepherd and making his ministry to his sheep effective and helpful. Jesus said, "My sheep . . . shall never perish, neither shall any man pluck them out of my hand" (John 10:27-28). The Good Shepherd, too, uses rod and staff. We cannot see them, but we know that no harm can come to those who are under His care. And we are comforted, living without fear or dread. Comfort is one of the treasures of the Shepherd.

THOU PREPAREST A TABLE

The great concept held in the mind of the poet is too big to be properly presented in one metaphor. Claiming to be a sheep in the shepherd's fold is only a part of the picture. To bring out the full meaning of his idea, the psalmist moves over into the realm of the human and represents himself as a guest at the banquet table of the divine Host. He is more than Jehovah's sheep. He is Jehovah's guest. It is daring to claim the intimacy which is suggested by this figure, but it is wholly in keeping with the development of the thought already presented. The Host in the banquet hall is the same loved friend as the Shepherd he has known. The picture of the feast is more realistic and comes nearer home to human understanding. After all, sheep are far from human. There is no fellowship and communication between sheep and shepherd such as is possible between host and guest, the Creator and one created in His image. The Host is our Father. We are His children. The family circle is set up.

The Oriental host was obligated to protect his guests. The heavenly Host carries out the same rigid procedure of protection that David has described in the Shepherd.

Our Lord took up this same attractive idea (cf. Luke 14) in His teaching and compared the Christian life to full enjoyment at a divinely set banquet table. Such bountiful preparation has been God's way all through the centuries. Notice the words *thou preparest a table for me*. The word *arak* is to "arrange with loving care." Foresight, understanding, and personal consideration enter into the preparation. Enemies may be on every hand and reason for haste may be apparent, but everywhere the guest finds ample provision for all his needs. This attention to every need is a beautiful touch revealing the heart of the Shepherd Host.

Thou anointest my head with oil. The people of the East made much of the anointing oil. The hearty welcome of the host is expressed in the lavish ointments and oils that are brought to put on the guest's head. You will remember Jesus' pathetic words, "My head with oil thou didst not anoint" (Luke 7:46). To Him there was a significant neglect. David assures us that the divine Host comes with the full welcome and with an implied dedication of His guest. The heads of kings, prophets, and priests were anointed to show that they were signally honored and solemnly consecrated to divine service. The lavish anointing which Mary of Bethany poured on the head of our Lord brought refreshment, joy, and deep satisfaction to the heart of the Saviour. David makes it clear that the one who has Jehovah as his host can be sure of continued mercies that will gladden the heart all the way home.

My cup runneth over. It is like God to give lavishly and unstintingly. The feast with him is a joyous occasion. His supply for his guests' needs is unlimited. The heart of the Giver has no thought or inclination toward stinginess or selfishness. Lavish giving and joyous bestowing of good things are in evidence in every movement of the divine hand. We cannot begin to estimate the wealth thus lavished upon us. We are helpless in counting up the cost of this elaborate feast provided for us. The mind is staggered by the richness and delicious quality of the divine gifts.

> The King of love my Shepherd is,
> Whose goodness faileth never;
> I nothing lack if I am His,
> And He is mine forever.
>
> Where streams of living water flow,
> My ransom'd soul He leadeth;
> And where the verdant pastures grow,
> With food celestial feedeth.
>
> Perverse and foolish, oft I stray'd,
> But yet in love He sought me,
> And on His shoulder gently laid,
> And home rejoicing brought me.
>
> In death's dark vale I fear no ill,
> With Thee, dear Lord, beside me;
> Thy rod and staff my comfort still,
> Thy cross before to guide me.

Thou spread'st a table in my sight,
Thy unction grace bestoweth;
And, oh, what transport of delight
With which my cup o'erfloweth.

HENRY W. BAKER

Goodness and mercy pursue me. All the believer's days are
to be characterized by the unwearying pursuit of two faithful messengers commissioned by the Shepherd. These two
guardian angels, *Goodness* and *Mercy*, will never leave him
for an instant. The divine Shepherd leads on. The heavenly
escort will follow all the way. These twin angels of God
will never sleep, never fail, never prove inadequate. They
are a part of the provision of a loving God who has determined to give personal, individual help at every moment all
life through. The knowledge of his concern is breath taking!

These two messengers are, in reality, the personified at-
tributes of God, *his goodness* and *his mercy.* They are God
in action. Both of them are necessary. These two faithful
helpers pursue every one of the Shepherd's own, whispering
words of comfort, placing strong arms about the weak, res-
cuing those who have slipped, bringing back those who have
strayed, and empowering each one for richer and fuller living
on the journey through life's difficult way. "The eternal God
is thy refuge, and underneath are the everlasting arms"
(Deut. 33:27).

AND I WILL DWELL

The psalmist has assured us over and over again of the
certainty of rich blessings every step of our earthly journey.
We are not to want for rest, refreshment, restoration, guidance, protection, fellowship, comfort, or any other need one
can know. He realizes how powerful within us is the desire
for permanence, for something that will endure on into the

life beyond the grave. He has described the love of God in action and has declared that no earthly need will ever go unsatisfied. He now takes another step and makes it clear that the Shepherd does not desert us in the hour of death. The love of God does not fail us. In a moment of climax he dares claim a home at the end of the way.

Forever is a long time. Eternity is wrapped within it. The eternal Shepherd, who watches over us every second of the earthly journey, has a richer, a surer, a grander boon for His own. The royal palace is a special creation for those who have been kept, blessed, and led by His loving hand. When the rough way is over, the child of God will find the riches of fellowship forever with the Shepherd.

Jesus calls it "my Father's house." He makes it clear that the provisions stored up for us there are more glorious than eye can see or heart comprehend. He would call us out to purer living, more obedient following, more fervent praying, more dynamic witnessing, and happier fellowship as we prepare for our enjoyment of the heavenly home.

I will dwell in the house of the Lord forever.

First Corinthians XIII

Though I speak with the tongues of men and of angels, and have not love, I am become as sounding brass, or a tinkling cymbal. And though I have the gift of prophecy, and understand all mysteries, and all knowledge; and though I have all faith, so that I could remove mountains, and have not love, I am nothing. And though I bestow all my goods to feed the poor, and though I give my body to be burned, and have not love, it profiteth me nothing.

Love suffereth long, and is kind; love envieth not; love vaunteth not itself, is not puffed up, doth not behave itself unseemly, seeketh not her own, is not . . . provoked, thinketh no evil; rejoiceth not in iniquity, but rejoiceth in the truth; beareth all things, believeth all things, hopeth all things, endureth all things.

Love never faileth: but whether there be prophecies, they shall fail; whether there be tongues, they shall cease; whether there be knowledge, it shall vanish away. For we know in part, and we prophesy in part. But when that which is perfect is come, then that which is in part shall be done away. When I was a child, I spake as a child, I understood as a child, I thought as a child: but when I became a man, I put away childish things. For now we see through a glass, darkly; but then face to face: now I know in part; but then shall I know even as also I am known. And now abideth faith, hope, love, these three; but the greatest of these is love.

III. How Love Behaves

_____*First Corinthians XIII*

HOW EXQUISITELY BEAUTIFUL and how unspeakably sublime is this thirteenth chapter of First Corinthians. This precious poem of surpassing beauty stands as the deepest and strongest production of the pen of Paul. No golden sunset or lovely strain of music has ever approached it in sheer beauty. But the remarkable value of these verses, however, is in their power to grip the human mind and will and bring about a full turning back to the Son of God. How we would like to measure up to the picture that Paul shows us here! As we are gripped by this challenge, let us turn to our Lord in genuine dedication of all that we are and can ever be.

In chapters twelve, thirteen, and fourteen of his first letter to the Corinthians Paul presented the subject of spiritual gifts. In chapter twelve he described the rich treasures the people of Corinth had in these gifts. In chapter thirteen the vital energy of these endowments was revealed. In chapter fourteen he encouraged the people to exercise these gifts in a worthy manner. This beautiful thirteenth chapter rests quietly and serenely between the noise and tumult and divisions of the Corinthian church. Desiring and exercising gifts are both important, but the Corinthian Christians must realize that the one true way of life is the way of love.

Some of the excellent outlines used by older commentators may be stated as follows: 1–3, the values of love; 4–7, the characteristics of love; 8–13, the permanence of love; 1–3, love contrasted; 4–7, love analyzed; 8–13, love defended; 1–3, love's pre-eminence; 4–7, love's prerogatives; 8–13, love's permanence; 1–3, a brilliant life with love left out; 4–7, a beautiful life with love in evidence; 8–13, a blessed life wherein love is permanent. It is interesting to see that each has found the same divisions and has sensed the same great ideas.

The word "love" calls for special treatment. Paul used a word, *agape,* that is truly a New Testament word. The Septuagint used it only once. There are three words in the Greek language which can be translated "love." The first of them, *eros,* describes passion, lust, sensual desire. It is not used in the New Testament. The second word, *philos,* tells of the natural love of personal affection, of impulse, of our human love for one another. The third word, *agape,* denotes an affection that is well above the area of spontaneous emotion and describes the Christian love that is like the love of God. The will enters into the choice of the object of love, and the result is a self-denying devotion that is unique. The New Testament has lifted the idea of *agape* into a higher, cleaner, and more unselfish atmosphere.

Jerome, in his translation of the Bible into Latin, used *caritas* instead of *amor* because the latter word had taken on sensual connotations. When Wycliffe translated this word into English, he used the word "charity." The King James' translation did the same; thus we have had the word "charity" for hundreds of years. In time, the meaning of the word "charity" has changed so that it is now wholly inadequate. To express the rich meaning recorded by Paul, we must translate *agape* as "love" and think of the rich, strong, self-sacrificing love of our Lord and Saviour.

A LIFE WITHOUT LOVE (1–3)

The poet turns portrait painter and outlines on the canvas before our eyes a remarkable picture of a brilliant person who has every known endowment and every possible equipment. The imagination runs riot as the full list of unusual and incredible strands of greatness appear before us. How can any man possess such great qualities? How can anyone attain such heights? The artist makes us admire him extravagantly and then, without warning, tells us that the one single ingredient that alone can guarantee true greatness is missing. Not one single bit of love can be found. Not one ounce of worth can be discovered. The life is useless. The total value of the individual is an absolute zero.

The portrait reveals first an eloquent speaker with every demand of elocution, rhetoric, and oratory fully satisfied in a display of spellbinding eloquence. The whole production fell flat and useless. The orator was as disappointingly valueless. His "perfect" masterpiece had failed. He was a mere instrument without color, without personality, without power, because love was absent. He was only a big noise. Discord, raucous blaring of jangling noises, ear-splitting sounds without meaning, and unproductive effort were the full result of the efforts of his expenditure of energy. Without love the result is ever so.

The second stroke of the brush reveals a man who, like Balaam, had insight into God's plans for His people and who could make predictions with startling accuracy. In addition to this power, he could peer into the mysteries understood only by the divine One and reveal the full meaning of those things to his contemporaries. Moreover, he had stored up in his mind all the knowledge that was available, properly catalogued and related so that it was instantly available. How could a man have such superhuman powers and equipment? With all these things he possessed a faith that equipped him to cope with life and its difficulties without ever losing a critical engagement. His was a wonder-working faith that was able to claim miraculous victories.

Imagine the apostle's verdict on a man who has all these unusual and rare gifts. Listen to him: *and have not love . . . nothing*. All these things add up to zero. Love could have produced the mightiest life on the globe. Without that ingredient all went for naught. Even one who could discern the full counsel of God, interpret it fully to the people, and exercise miracle-working faith was utterly lacking in value. Without love he was worthless.

Even in his devotion to others this man measured up exceedingly well. There are two proofs of his devotion. He was unusually generous in placing all his goods at the disposal of the poor—even putting food into their mouths, piece by piece. He was conceivably so devoted to the cause of Christ that he was willing to take his own body as a special offering and put it on the altar of fire. But when the test was made, not one small bit of love was discovered. As a consequence, every outward act of generosity and even fanatical offering was utterly useless. No value could be found in this man's life. It was a total failure, for no love was there.

It is clear then that love is greater than eloquence, prophecy, wisdom, knowledge, faith, charity, and martyrdom. These have no value apart from love, but love adds great value to these highly prized gifts. When love that is spiritual, divine, and indestructible controls heart, mind, will, and choices, the fruits are eternally valuable (Gal. 5:2–23).

A LIFE WITH LOVE (4–7)

Another portrait is presented in which the qualities or virtues of love are pictured. In this portrait the signs, qualities, marks, properties, fruits, and characteristics of love are revealed. Dr. Graham Scroggie insists that verses 1–3 give us a picture of what the church at Corinth was and should not have been, while verses 4–7 show what that church was not but should be. The first is a picture of gifts without love, and the second is a view of love without gifts. In arriving at this exquisite paragraph, the author does not depend on the dream of an artist but upon the work of a photographer. The Lord Jesus is the subject of this picture. To love like this is to be like Him.

Suffers long: Patience under suffering and misfortune is a noble quality that is born of love. Under offenses, injuries, and stress love has a way of proving its true worth. It is slow to lose patience. It is silent as days and nights pass and the pressure increases. Whatever the provocation, the load, or the pressure, love will always prove that the way ahead is a glorious one. It understands, and therefore waits.

Is kind: It is possible to find people in the world who are unkind, but one certain conclusion is that love does not dwell in their lives. Love creates an atmosphere in which kindness can grow. Considerateness, thoughtfulness, and gentleness of soul will be evident when love provides the soil for their growth. Kindness is an active quality, giving itself away in unselfish deeds. Kind things are done by people who have love in their hearts.

Envieth not: Envy is an ugly word. Can you imagine anything worse than envy? The word carries the idea of "boiling"—all "heated up" and restless under the pressure of selfishness and hatred. To envy is to dislike excellence in others. It is the vice most thoroughly despised and the last one to die. Paul tells us that envy cannot live in the rare atmosphere made sweet and clean by the presence of love. It is good to know that there is at least one remedy that can be depended on to kill the offensive pest known as envy. Generosity and magnanimity rule in the heart where love resides. Love allows neither envy nor jealousy to live in its presence.

Vaunteth not itself: The word "itself" is a key word here. The modesty which love produces does not allow room for vainglory or self-boasting. Such modesty does not brag. It does not have inflated ideas of its own importance. Selfish pride cannot grow. Conceit is altogether out of the question. Boasting does not come from the heart where love lives.

Not puffed up: The verb "puffed" is formed from the word *phusa*, which means "bellows." Paul declares that love refuses to puff itself out like a pair of bellows. Bragging and conceit are out of order. Again we look upon Jesus as the true example of this striking quality. How truly He showed the way for sweet humility of spirit! Love does not call attention to itself as worthy of notice.

Doth not behave itself unseemly: Love is never rude. How could it be impolite or unmannerly? Courtesy and considerateness are always present where love reigns. A gentle spirit always manifests the kind of courteous thoughtfulness that reveals the fact that love is in control. How we do need the power of love in all our lives to keep us from being rude!

Seeketh not her own: How could we expect love to be guilty of selfish seeking? All through His full life Jesus gave a demonstration of love incarnate that never sought its own interests. He was constantly proving that love gives itself freely that others might live.

Is not provoked: How does love behave when cruel irrita-

tion is confronted? Paul dares tell us that love *is not provoked.*
The old translators slipped in the little word "easily" to
soften Paul's rigid requirement. There is no basis for the
addition in any of the ancient manuscripts. The words must
be read exactly as Paul wrote them. How many times have
you excused yourself for an ugly display of temper on the
strength of the little word "easily"? Paul declares that love
is not "touchy," is not swift to blaze into anger. John and
James were fighters until love came to live in their hearts.
What a difference love makes! If you are irritable and
"touchy," let love come in to change the whole picture. The
Lord Jesus showed the way, manifesting love in thought and
word and deed.

Thinketh no evil: A literal rendering of these words
might be "taking not account of evil." The picture is that of
one who does not carry a notebook or ledger to record every
wrong, slight, or hurt so that he may "get even" with the one
doing the wrong. He has no desire to keep account of real
or imaginary wrongs. Instead, he always enjoys granting forgiveness. He can "forgive and forget." He never harbors
a grudge, never broods over any slight. Lincoln was unusual
in this particular. It is said of him that he never forgot a
kindness and that he had no room in his mind for the memory of a wrong. He had a forgiving spirit. It is tragic to
find David, at the close of his life, remembering the wrongs
done him by Joab and Shimei. He had stored up those
wrongs through the years. They had added misery to his
life. Love does not keep such records.

Rejoiceth not . . . rejoiceth: Dr. James Moffatt's translation of this verse reads: "Love is never glad when others go
wrong, love is . . . always eager to believe the best." Love
finds the right occasion for rejoicing. How could one be
happy over the triumphs of injustice? Love hates sin and

grieves over it, never finding pleasure in witnessing wrong on its way to triumph. Love sides with truth always. Love can always be counted on to stand solidly against injustice and as powerfully alongside truth. Love is gladdened by goodness. Love is also a good test of character. It reveals much when it reveals what one favors.

Beareth all things: This verb may carry the idea of enduring hardships, troubles, and indignities, or it can take meaning from its root word, "roof." Love covers, protects, shields. Love will receive on itself the blows intended for another. It will gladly take the brunt of the attack and save the one loved from embarrassment or pain. Love knows no limit to its endurance in bearing for others. It bravely stands up to life and gladly chooses to suffer, to bear, and to carry.

Believeth all things: Love has faith in men. These words do not imply that love is foolishly gullible but that there is a full supply of faith in human hearts that have been touched by the Master. Love is not suspicious. There is nothing of the cynic, the pessimist, the slanderer, or the defamer in love. Trustfulness is a good trait. It grows out of love. Some of us have never forgotten the grip of a strong hand and the sincere voice of a strong man saying, "Boy, I believe in you." Eternity alone will reveal the tremendous effect on such a young life. Love believes in people. It is willing to give the benefit of the doubt and to keep on trusting.

Hopeth all things: This hopefulness is a mighty thing. Jesus was constantly bringing amazement to men with his optimistic hope for all sorts of individuals. There were no impossible cases with Him. He knew what was in man. He could see hidden virtues, untapped resources, and eternal qualities that made for a profound hope. In spite of evidence that seemed conclusive, He continued to have faith in the individual.

Endureth all things: Even when it receives that which it does not deserve, love can bear up with sweet grace and unending strength. Love carries on in sunshine and in shade, in prosperity and in adversity, in all the changing scenes of life. Steadfast and unmoved, love faces injuries and burdens and carries them with sublime fortitude. An enduring soul is led on daily by the strength that comes from love's presence. How beautifully perseverance was exemplified in the life of our Lord! All the way to Calvary He continued His devoted journey, always seeking the way to bring life, joy, and peace to others.

In summary, let us quote Dr. Graham Scroggie:

We must all acknowledge then that love is the greatest of all great things of the world; not hasty, but patient; not inconsiderate, but benevolent; not envious, but content; not boastful, but unostentatious; not arrogant, but humble; not rude, but courteous; not selfish, but self-forgetful; not irritable, but good-tempered; not vindictive, but generous; not malevolent, but high-principled; not rebellious, but brave; not suspicious, but confident; not despondent, but undiscouragable; not conquerable, but indomitable.[1]

THE PERMANENCE OF LOVE (8–13)

Love never faileth: Here is the heart of this sublime hymn. "Never" is a long time. Love is imperishable. No end can ever come to love. There is nothing partial, passing, or transient about it. It never falls to the ground in defeat. It never fails to reach the full completion of its purpose. It is of God and is as eternal as God Himself. It survives everything. This little sentence summarizes all that Paul has pre-

---

[1] *The Keswick Week, 1935,* p. 122.

sented. Love began with God; it will go on through all
eternity.

Prophecies . . . done away: The old Greek verb means "to
make idle" or "inoperative." All these special gifts designed
for man's instruction will pass off the stage when they have
accomplished that for which they were created. They are
only temporary. The special gift of prophecy will be possessed by all; there will be no need for a select group to
have it. All shall dwell in God's unveiled presence, and such
gifts shall give place to something higher.

Tongues shall cease: When these gifts have finished their
assigned task and there is no longer any need for them,
they will automatically cease. When all believers speak the
language of ecstasy, there will be no need for this special
phenomenon. The transient and passing will be completely
ended.

Knowledge . . . done away: Even the remarkable gift of
knowledge will be no longer necessary. It is amazing how
much of the knowledge we have is of a temporary character. It
will all pass off the stage, wholly superseded by new knowledge that comes to be our possession.

In part: Paul declares that our knowledge and our proph-
esying are necessarily partial, incomplete, and imperfect.
Even the best mind among us has received only a small
part of the whole store of knowledge. His understanding of
that knowledge is far from being full and perfect, and his
interpretation of that knowledge to others (prophecy) is
even more partial, limited, and imperfect.

Perfect: A day is coming when the perfect (the mature,
the full grown, the complete) will be in effect. That day
will be God's gift, showing the fullest and richest realization
of the eternal revelation. Paul hastens to assure the readers

of the epistle that in that day, which is certain to come, the partial, the imperfect, and the incomplete will be seen to flower into God's most perfect manifestation of knowledge, wisdom, and divine revelation. What a day that will be! The partial will be absorbed into or superseded by the fullest of God's creations. No one will need or miss the old things in the splendor of the perfect. Understanding and knowledge are progressive. They are ever expanding, growing, and maturing. The partial prepares for and moves toward the perfect. God works by means of that which is passing to prepare the way for the eternal and the full display of His mighty purpose for His creatures.

When I was a child: Paul illustrates these statements by telling of his own experience of growing in knowledge and understanding. As a tiny baby his knowledge was very limited. In those early days he prattled baby talk as an infant is expected to do. He says, "I used to talk . . . I used to understand. I used to reason or calculate as a baby." Those judgments of his childhood were not, in any sense, to be compared with adult decisions. They were not untrue or wrong, but they were inadequate and incomplete.

I became an adult: Then something happened! Paul grew up. He claims that he brought to an end the baby way of talking, understanding, and making decisions. He began to live on a new plane with new equipment and to produce better decisions. In the same way, Paul says, the ignorance and partial understanding of spiritual things that each person exhibits now is to become a miracle-working experience in the new day. All will be new. All will be higher. All will be on a heavenly plane. The spiritual gifts these Christians have so far enjoyed belong to the state of spiritual childhood on earth. When Christ comes again, spiritual maturity will be attained and these things will be made inoperative. Inadequate apprehension will give place to full understanding in His holy presence.

Mirror . . . darkly: Ancient mirrors were made of polished metal and not of glass. It was never possible to get distinct images. The word "obscurely" would be a better translation than "darkly." In this world there is only an inadequate, imperfect, and partial view of things. Vision will be much better on the other shore. The indirect mode of apprehension will give place to the immediate and the direct, for seeing face to face will make clear understanding possible. There will be the immediate vision that makes clear all the features and all the angles. The knowledge that has been suited to the earthly state will be out of the question for those who receive the heavenly knowledge. Entire new fields of knowledge will be opened up to eager minds. God will be known in a marvelous way. It sounds almost too good to be true. Paul gives us full assurance by the authority of the Holy Spirit that these things will be.

Faith, hope, love: The gifts mentioned above—prophecy, tongues, and knowledge—will pass away and will remain permanently discarded, but these three—faith, hope, and love—shall abide eternally. All three of these are to remain and have place in all the vast reaches of eternity. In no sense will any of the three become useless or needless. However full the new life with God may become, there will always be a place for faith, hope, and love. Unchanged and permanent, they are to be the precious possession of the redeemed ones in glory.

Faith will become clearer, stronger, richer, and more satisfying than we can imagine. Absolute dependence and happy confidence will find keener expression than ever before in our lives. *Hope* abides. At every turn in the road the believer can look expectantly for vistas of eternal beauty, for adventures to delight the heart, for evidence of the divine arm about him, for joys that are indescribable, for breath-taking moments of praise and awe and worship, and for soul-satisfying delights as the Saviour leads and lifts and blesses.

Love, the greatest of these: God is love! From the beginning of this lovely poem Paul has been singing of the excellencies and golden qualities of love. He has shown us what it will do in a human life, what fruits it will produce, and what exquisite fragrance it brings into a world so full of need. It is eternal. It is the greatest of the eternal graces.

Follow after love: The first verse of the fourteenth chapter is a call to strenuous action with everything keyed and dedicated to the one job of living a love-mastered life. Such a life will pay big dividends. It will make for joy. It will bring forth the choicest fruits to the glory of our Lord and Saviour. It will bring joy to His heart.

Psalm LI

Have mercy upon me, O God, according to thy lovingkindness: according unto the multitude of thy tender mercies blot out my transgressions. Wash me thoroughly from mine iniquity, and cleanse me from my sin. For I acknowledge my transgressions: and my sin is ever before me. . . . Purge me with hyssop, and I shall be clean: wash me, and I shall be whiter than snow. Make me to hear joy and gladness; that the bones which thou hast broken may rejoice. Hide thy face from my sins, and blot out all mine iniquities. Create in me a clean heart, O God; and renew a right spirit within me. Cast me not away from thy presence; and take not thy holy spirit from me. Restore unto me the joy of thy salvation; and uphold me with thy free spirit. Then will I teach transgressors thy ways: and sinners shall be converted unto thee. Deliver me from bloodguiltiness, O God, thou God of my salvation: and my tongue shall sing aloud of thy righteousness.

IV. The Way Home

Psalm LI

GOD'S GREAT AND GOOD MAN had fallen into grievous sin. He was frightfully out of touch with his God. Misery and remorse of conscience had been his daily portion. Anxious fears came to make him imagine that he would be banished from the presence of the holy One. Life had become increasingly unbearable for the sinner. All his rationalization left him more clearly in the wrong and more completely abandoned by his God. David had known and loved God. His sensitive soul had ever been aware of the presence of One who loved him and who sought to have him near. Now unrest, uneasiness, and agony of soul were his constant companions. Life was not the same. The music had gone out of his soul. He wanted relief. He wanted God. How could it be? How was he to find God?

Do we hear the stifled sobs of multitudes who have lost touch with God and who are miserable beyond compare? Are there men, young and old, who would give any price to come back to the strong arms of God and feel the grip of His love about them? Perhaps you are one of them. Have you slipped away from the Father's hand so that miseries fill your soul? You will want to follow closely and watch as

God's great and good man finds his way out of sin, guilt, soul agony, and restless uselessness into the clear light of a full victory. David the sinner becomes David the ardent singer. You may find the victory, too.

PUNGENT PREACHING

Nathan knew about David's sin. He knew how helplessly David was struggling. He knew of the loneliness of the king's heart as he was forced to go along out of tune with God. He knew how utterly helpless the poor sinner was as he continued to count on his own efforts to bring peace of mind. Fearlessly, personally, pointedly, and skilfully the preacher confronted the sinner. First he presented a story that aroused the king's wrath and brought from him an angry order of execution for the cruel neighbor in the story. What a blind spot David revealed! Then with dramatic suddenness Nathan drove the stiletto home: "Thou art the man!" David accepted the sermon directed to his heart. God had spoken. Conviction gripped the sinner.

THE KING'S SEARCH

The king knew that he must find his way back to God. But how? He was only one of countless millions of all races who have sought to find God and have peace with Him. David was a king and a wealthy man. Countless cattle and goats were his to offer as sacrifices. Olive oil in a mighty stream could be poured out. The priests and Levites were at his bidding. But all these earthly remedies seemed only the poorest stubble beside that which he needed. He was out of touch with God. He had sinned sins that put him outside the reach of all offerings available to man. He must go directly to God to ask for pardon, cleansing, and restoration.

THE KING'S HUMILITY

In deep reverence of soul, pull aside the curtain to David's inner chamber and watch him as he talks to God. No other point of view will let this psalm come to life. Watch him as he goes into the secret place to be alone with God. Hear him as he begs and pleads, confesses and implores, promises and vows his inner soul to the God who had been precious to him in other days. His prayer is an urgent plea for grace, cleansing, restoration, and re-creation. Listen to the deepest yearnings of his inner heart and to his sacred vows to God. Having faced self, and having seen his own sins in all their hideousness, he felt genuine concern and a strong desire for pardon and cleansing. He was thoroughly conscious of his own helplessness and was willing to turn to God.

A PLEA FOR FORGIVENESS (1, 2)

Even before he named his sins, David called out to God for forgiveness. Can you conceive of any need that man has that can compare in importance with this need for divine forgiveness? God's mercy must be received before anything else matters in this life or in the ages of eternity. David called loudly and insistently for mercy, for God's full grace. The Hebrew verbs *hanan* and *raham* have to do with an earnest call for compassion, mercy, and the bestowal of undeserved favor. David was appealing to God because he wisely recognized Him as the giver of the only mercy that could suffice. David had known Jehovah in earlier days and had found Him to be a God of mercy. He was sure now that he could confidently beg for divine mercy.

The three words David used for sin and the three words he used for forgiveness (cf. Psalm 32) not only reveal his keen understanding of the true nature of sin and the way of salvation, but they also show his sense of God's eternal willingness to work a miracle for the unworthy soul of one of His sinning creatures. Let us study these words:

Pesha (transgression) reveals a rebellious heart that defiantly goes counter to the will of God. David had rebelled against God. No subject of the divine kingdom could with impunity be guilty of such an act of high treason. It was unthinkable that God's greatest leader was guilty of this crime. David admitted that he was the sinner. He knew that he stood guilty in the eyes of God.

Awon (iniquity) is the state into which a heart has come because of sin. It is a warped or twisted or depraved state of mind and heart. What a tragic picture of sin's power! The great king was willing to plead guilty to that condition of heart.

Hatah (sin) reveals a pathetic failure on the part of the sinner to measure up to the divine purpose and blueprint for his life. It has to do with "missing the mark." How tragically David had missed the mark! How God had counted on him from his early days on the hills of Bethlehem! This word must have brought hot tears to his face as he recognized the sorry mess he had made.

As you look back on your own life, can you find evidences of these conditions? Have you rebelled against God's will? Do you recognize your life as twisted, knotted, warped, and depraved? As you look carefully at God's blueprint and specifications for your life, are you shamefully aware of failure, blunder, and "missing the mark"? Do you wonder that David begged for forgiveness and for the tender mercy of God?

Mahah (blot out) signifies an erasing of all the lines in that ugly record. No human hand could reach them or erase them. Only God's hand had access to this record and the

power to remove it forever from the book. David pleaded
with God for the miraculous touch that would make this
change. The ugly record could be canceled.

Kavas (wash) is a rough word. The cleansing which it
indicates would not be easy or pleasant; instead, it would
be exceedingly painful. Such cleansing was necessary, however; the psalmist realized that nothing short of a clean heart,
mind, and body could ever be acceptable in God's sight. He
was seeking access to the presence of God. He wanted
cleansing that would fit him for that sacred place.

Taher (cleanse) has to do with the ritual pronouncement
indicating full approval for entrance into a worship service.
Again and again David came back to this idea. He hated
sin with holy hatred. He wanted no trace or vestige or
smell of it left on his soul or his body. He knew that the
holy God could not countenance sin in any form, and was
determined to have his sin removed through the only way
available. He appealed to the heart of a merciful God for
forgiving and cleansing, for that which would make him fit
again.

AN HONEST CONFESSION (3–6)

It is never easy to open the heart in a full and sincere
confession. It was probably more difficult for David to do
this than for the ordinary person. He was God's anointed.
He had been the spiritual leader of his people as well as
their earthly sovereign. He had composed their sacred poetry
and had organized the ritual for public worship.

He had carried this sin of his for a year while going on
with his direction of the worship of the nation. During these
months he had manufactured all grades of excuses and
human explanations for his despicable conduct. He had tried
to convince himself that all was well. Not one line of confes-

sion had escaped his lips, for confession was not easy. It was
something new, something strangely different from any
other word of his. In his humiliation and agony he was able
to see that it was the one and only way to victory, peace,
and forgiveness. It is still God's way for every sinning soul.
It is still difficult and embarrassing. Men still shun it as
they seek easier solutions. Are you one of these?

*I acknowledge my transgressions: and my sin is ever be-
fore me:* Nathan had said, "Thou art the man." David said,
"I am the man." Day and night he had lived with the con-
sciousness of that foul sin within his heart. He faced God
now with his forthright confession. Nothing was held back.
No extenuating circumstance was blamed. Bathsheba might
have been wrong in some indiscretion or careless conduct,
but the psalmist did not allow her name to carry any of the
blame. No one among his associates could be charged with
any of his guilt. No reference was made to low standards,
contemporary behavior, or worldly custom. None of these
could have any of the blame. David manfully and sincerely
confessed his sin to God.

In this confession we are face to face with genuine repentance. It is strangely akin to that New Testament concept
found in the word *metanoieo.* There is nothing superficial
or purely outward in this experience. David was deeply
moved by a sense of guilt. He was fully aware of God's
hatred of sin and God's imperious demands on the sinner.
In sheer honesty he bared the inner depths of his soul, and
from those depths he spoke his heart's deepest truth. In
dealing with a holy God he could do no less. He was truly
penitent, and from a contrite heart came his pathetic confession. How we do need such penitence in our public and
private confessions today! How transforming our experiences could be if this significant step could be taken! David

walked the way of conviction, repentance, and confession to full forgiveness, restoration, and usefulness.

THE CLEANSING TOUCH (7)

David was still conscious of his heart's defilement. Forgiveness was a precious boon and he valued it highly, but he needed more than that. In addition to merciful forgiveness, he begged for the touch of God's hand to make him clean. This plaintive plea must have pleased God. Are you conscious of the need of cleansing? Does it strike you as a necessary step in the road that leads back toward pleasing God?

Hata (purge) David also knew that God alone could make him white and clean again. He knew that God was the One to sprinkle him with hyssop branches so that he could be certified as ceremonially clean.

Kavas (wash) Another full washing by the divine hand would guarantee that his soul would glisten like the whitest snow in all the earth. The prophet Isaiah must have remembered this line when he wrote, "Though your sins be as scarlet, they shall be as white as snow; though they be red like crimson, they shall be as wool" (Isa. 1:18). Why are we satisfied with less than the whitest? How can we settle for less than the best that God has to offer? Life is short— eternity is long. He has the highest gifts waiting for the repentant sinner. It will please Him greatly if we pray David's prayer.

JOY BELLS (8)

David was keenly conscious of a tragic lack in his life. The music had gone out of his heart. The joy bells had become silent. Joy was a thing of the past. Life has so much of the drab, the drudgery, the humdrum, the unpleasant.

How can one afford to live without music, singing, joy, and praise as he continues his way? The psalmist knew that for him such existence was out of the question. He had come step by step along the way to God's highest for him. He now broke forth into pleading that joy, gladness, and singing might be his again. Such a request would be mere presumption at any court in the world except at the throne of God. He was talking to the One who made such a life possible. Again how do you measure up? Have you found the joy and gladness that our Lord and Saviour alone can give? Nothing short of the fullest grasp of this heavenly boon is worthy of one who claims to be God's child. It is a glorious certainty through God's Son.

TRANSGRESSIONS' REMOVAL (9)

Who wants old, dead, forgiven sins lying around in plain sight while the new man goes joyously about the beautiful job of living? David certainly wanted to be rid of them. He knew he was talking to the One who could put them out of sight forever. He knew that he did not want God to see those old sins, these evidences of a depraved, twisted, warped inner nature. He was now on the highroad. None of these evidences of failure, rebellion, and depravity were in place. Have you prayed as fervently that such things might be annihilated by the strong hand of our Lord? The Master stands ready to give the answer and the victory (Psalm 103: 10–14).

A NEW CREATURE (10–12)

David discovered the destructive power of sin. He saw how pathetically a heart was ruined when sin reigned there. Repairs were out of the question, and God alone could provide a new heart. The psalmist asked for a new creative act on the part of the Creator; the same verb, *bara,* was used in the dawn of creation. God must supply the power and make a new creature. David was giving expression to the germ of the idea of the new birth. It would find its fuller meaning in the light of New Testament teachings, but the old poet, one thousand years before Christ, looked into the meaning of what Paul called the "new creature in Christ."

A SACRED VOW (13–15)

David responded like any Christian and caught the spirit of a redeemed saint. He declared that he would instantly set about doing the most obvious thing imaginable: he would seek out those miserable creatures of the earth who needed the salvation he had experienced. He would *teach them* (*lamad*) the successive steps in the way back to God. He would tell them of his own misery, his want, his need, his spiritual poverty. He would reveal to them God's part in the soul experience. He would lead them to see themselves and then to see God as He is. With talking, singing, a glowing radiance, and an irrepressible happiness that set joy bells going he would stay with them until they took those individual steps back to God. One by one he would find them, teach them, woo them, and win them. The message of the cross guarantees exactly this: reconciliation with God and transformation of lives.

Preaching, singing, teaching, and witnessing are still the God-given directions for winning lost men and women. David was on the right track. We must want them, waylay them, walk with them, warn them, woo them, and win them. David made it clear that only those who have come step by step as he had come would be effective. The Holy Spirit leads the way in preparing us for the task and in convicting the ones to whom we go.

AN UNQUESTIONED CONFIDENCE (7,13–14)

David manifested an unusual amount of faith and assurance that the incredible requests he was making would be fulfilled completely and fully. It takes faith to pray like that. Even though he was making great demands on the grace of God, he seemed possessed with absolute assurance that the answer would come in its entirety. *Purge me . . . I shall be clean; wash me . . . I shall be whiter than snow.* He knew God so well that he was willing to believe that this great boon would be granted. He was to be clean. He was to be white again. God's miracle would be seen. The new man would emerge. The music in his soul would be ringing out again. Forgiveness, cleansing, and full restoration were as certain as the coming of the dawn. His testimony in word, song, and life would be fully effective and sinners would be brought back to God. God would answer his plea.

What a faith! What unquestioned assurance! You will note that David was not claiming any of these happy results because of any power or effort of his own. He admitted that they came through the miraculous working of the infinite grace of God. John Newton sang of this grace in his immortal hymn.

> Amazing grace! how sweet the sound,
> That saved a wretch like me!
> I once was lost, but now am found,
> Was blind, but now I see.

Your testimony and mine can be as great when we have become intimately acquainted with the eternal Giver of these blessings and when we have entered fully and minutely into each step of David's prayer. Are you eager for this confidence, this power, and these golden assurances? Let the Holy Spirit take over in your life, and let yourself go back to the starting point. From there you may mount up to the very summit of complete victory in Him.

Through His atoning death the Lord Jesus has forever set up that

> . . . fountain filled with blood
>   Drawn from Immanuel's veins;
> And sinners, plunged beneath that flood,
>   Lose all their guilty stains.
>
> WILLIAM COWPER

He wants to become our Saviour. Any person may have free salvation through simple faith in Him. By the power of the Holy Spirit he will find victories daily in his quest of the highest and purest. Our Saviour has said, "No man cometh unto the Father, but by me" (John 14:6), and, "Him that cometh to me I will in no wise cast out" (John 6:37). Paul said, "Believe on the Lord Jesus Christ, and thou shalt be saved" (Acts 16:31). How can any man anywhere reject certain salvation?

GOD'S REQUIREMENTS (16,17)

David paused at the close of his prayer. Even though there was a sacrificial system a few yards away, he realized that God would not accept those sacrifices as propitiation for his own ugly sins. They were wholly inadequate. The mass of guilt lying upon his soul was great. He wanted to be freed from it. Under the leadership of the Holy Spirit he came forth with these ageless words, *The sacrifices of God are a broken spirit: a broken and a contrite heart, O God, thou wilt not despise*. The kind of Godly sorrow for sin that brings about true repentance is the prescription written here. David is but recounting the moment-by-moment movement from misery to triumph which he had experienced. He had given a complete demonstration of God's requirements for any sinner. When each movement in this series is completed, the victory is complete. Faith brings the victory and the life.

By way of summary, it may be said that this psalm makes an impact on young and old if it is studied and understood as the agonizing heart-cry of one hopelessly trapped and completely helpless. In his prayer David went step by step through an unusually logical route to ultimate victory. Perhaps we may think of these steps as follows: the terrifying power and grip of sin, the amazing love and infinite mercy of God, the utter helplessness of the sinner, the amazing simplicity of the road back to God, the abounding assurance of full healing and cleansing, the enthusiastic response of the redeemed one, the eternal life through Jesus Christ as Saviour.

For you there is victory ahead. No one need live in sin, in shallow, selfish living, or in useless existence. Our eternal Father, through His Son, has provided victorious living for every one of us. Why not come back to Him in trust, in repentance, in hope, in sincere prayer, in glad expectancy, and in full surrender?

> There's a wideness in God's mercy,
> Like the wideness of the sea;
> There's a kindness in His justice,
> Which is more than liberty.
>
> There is welcome for the sinner,
> And more graces for the good;
> There is mercy with the Saviour;
> There is healing in His blood.

There is plentiful redemption
In the blood that has been shed;
There is joy for all the members
In the sorrows of the head.

For the love of God is broader
Than the measure of man's mind;
And the heart of the Eternal
Is most wonderfully kind.

FREDERICK W. FABER

Matthew V

Blessed are the poor in spirit: for theirs is the kingdom of heaven. Blessed are they that mourn: for they shall be comforted. Blessed are the meek: for they shall inherit the earth. Blessed are they which do hunger and thirst after righteousness: for they shall be filled. Blessed are the merciful: for they shall obtain mercy. Blessed are the pure in heart: for they shall see God. Blessed are the peacemakers: for they shall be called the children of God. Blessed are they which are persecuted for righteousness' sake: for theirs is the kingdom of heaven. . . .

Ye are the salt of the earth: but if the salt have lost his savour, wherewith shall it be salted? it is thenceforth good for nothing, but to be cast out, and to be trodden under foot of men. Ye are the light of the world. A city that is set on an hill cannot be hid. . . . Let your light so shine before men, that they may see your good works, and glorify your Father which is in heaven.

V. The Beatitudes

WHAT WOULD YOU GIVE for an authentic portrait of Jesus of Nazareth? It would be a priceless possession. How did He look? What was He like? Many artists have put forth their productions, which differ widely. We have no assurance that any of them is like Him. Our imagination will continue to run on in the vain hope that we can capture the features of that beloved face.

When Jesus set Himself to the task of describing the ideal man of His kingdom, we find Him painting a full-length, true-to-life portrait of Himself. It was natural for Him to put down the lineaments of a sublime character. To be good kingdom builders His representatives must have within their hearts the finer qualities that He possessed. Their characters, their thoughts, their attitudes, their loyalties, their words, and their deeds were to be exact replicas of the pattern He had lived in His earthly life. In this study of the Beatitudes we will watch with absorbing interest for the picture of Himself that our Lord Jesus put in imperishable lines to lure each Christian on to the heights of devoted living. We will be conscious of the fact that here is the ideal toward which He expects us to climb.

On every hand we meet the crushing realization that there is a pathetically low level of Christian living seen among believers who claim to be new creatures in Christ. Surely we see standards that are far below the high level which is God's purpose for us. We are seemingly satisfied with far too little Christian growth. We are content to approximate pagan or worldly standards. Spiritual food is available each day, and our Lord would have us eat of it and grow into stalwart men of God. These words from Jesus will exert a strong tonic effect upon us and pull us up for the days ahead.

The Sermon on the Mount (Matt. 5–7) is Christ's announcement to His apostles of His program for the conquest of the world. In it we find a clear, concise portrait of the kingdom man. That kingdom man is held before us while we look at his character, his influence, his conduct, and his destiny.

When we stop to think, we are reminded that Psalm 1 gives us the Old Testament text for this New Testament expository sermon. Jesus was thoroughly acquainted with the "Threshold Psalm" and realized that this biblical theme, which had been available for one thousand years, needed to be lived. He chose to ask His own disciples to put it into daily living and then to lead in the world emphasis on this brand of living. They were to set out before the world the eternal principles on which a godly life must be lived. They were to point the way by which true happiness could be found and enjoyed. Jesus had lived such a life. He now sought to have this exhibition of Christian living put squarely in the midst of life. His call to you and to me is that we shall join in this holy demonstration. The kingdom man is still the ideal toward which He bids us strive with all our being. The years have not dimmed the requirements which Jesus set up. They beckon to us as boldly as they did to the twelve.

THE SETTING

He went up into a mountain. It was a favorite way of the Master. He had a habit of going up into mountains. He spent nights alone among these familiar peaks as He prayed to the Father. His retreat was significant in this instance, for He was ready to challenge His followers with high and noble and heavenly ideals. He was determined to lift them to the heights. The people of the valleys, the hills, the cities, and the country were following Him in droves. They did not understand all that He had to say, but they were strangely stirred by His messages and drawn to Him for more.

All through the night He had been talking to His Father. In the early morning He had met with some of His most intimate followers and had called twelve of them to be apostles. They were to make preparation to take upon their shoulders the responsibilities of the kingdom. They needed training. They must now be introduced to the deeper principles of the kingdom. He was ready to enunciate the laws of His future rule among men. He sought to make clear to the disciples that character was the supreme requirement and that the individual must translate character into aggressive influence among the people of the earth.

He sat quietly and calmly, watching the rows of apostles and disciples as they came in closer to Him. His eyes then moved on out to the unusually large multitude that climbed the mountain to press very near Him. He was giving a special challenge to twelve men, but He was also speaking that message in language that took in all the members of that vast audience. The message was primarily for the apostles, but it was and is surprisingly directed to each of us, even to this day. When we become Christians, this picture of the ideal man comes to us with directness and freshness. We have been chosen by our Lord to live out the most minute teaching of our Lord's sermon.

THE BEATITUDES (3–12)

These exquisitely beautiful words are eternally true, pertinent, practical, and purposeful. Let us understand at the beginning that they are for believers. No one could think that such high standards could be expected for any except Christ's own inner family of redeemed souls. "Christians only" could be put as a placard on the exceptional requirements and upon the unusually rich promises accompanying these ideal demands. They are also pre-eminently designed for present living. They were to be lived that very afternoon as the apostles went down the hill into the crowded ways of life. They are for us today with that same call to immediate living. They certainly do not relate to some far-off day at His glorious coming. These laws and principles of the kingdom are to find individual response in those who are *in Christ.* We need to lean lovingly on the ministry of the Holy Spirit, who can make such living possible.

As we face the fact that the *King* of the kingdom is speaking to us, perhaps we should emphasize again the fact that only as one comes to Christ in personal trust and is born again can he be a member of His kingdom. Today much loose thinking prevails on entering the Master's kingdom. It is well to insist on full and complete surrender to the Holy Spirit to be made alive in Christ Jesus through the new birth. We are children of God, subjects of the King, regenerate individuals who are to be devoted to Him, eager to hear His demands, happy to do them, and ready immediately to walk as the Holy Spirit directs.

Blessed: What higher or more desirable concept can we

find? All men seek and have always sought something that strangely resembles this. Call it happiness, or soul prosperity, or God's constant care and watchfulness, or the heavenly bestowal of life's richest satisfactions, or anything else. All of us want it. We do not deserve it, but we will enjoy it and turn thankful hearts to the divine Giver.

What does "blessed" mean, then? Some would render it "happy." Certainly Jesus could both picture and demand happiness. No man ever had so much of it in his heart, voice, and face. Both Jesus and Paul made much of joy and happiness in their lives and teachings. The Greeks had a word (*eudamonia*) for human happiness. It was not equal to the strong word (*makarios*) used by our Lord in this discourse. Aristotle made the distinction when he used the stronger word to denote the blessedness which the Greeks considered an attribute or quality reserved for the gods. Jesus used the fuller term when He would unveil the portrait of the ideal citizen. It not only includes all the happiness that can be poured into it, but it also takes into account the divine approval and tender love that bring all of heaven's full satisfactions. The ideas suggested by the words "happy," "fortunate," "to be congratulated," and "blessed" are all to be blended into the picture Jesus intended.

We are immediately confronted with the thought that this peculiar gift from God is not bestowed upon any individual on the basis of unusual possessions or unusual activity or work. The reward is always on the basis of character. We may be sure that the Teacher was concerned with possessions and works. What a man had and what he did were matters that were important, but in this discourse the matter of real concern was the person himself. It will help to keep this distinction in mind.

Blessed are the poor in spirit (3): What a strange,

startling, and extraordinary statement this is! Is that what Jesus said? As He held out the keys to the kingdom, He began with this unexpected feature in the makeup of the ideal man. What does He mean? His idea certainly cannot be self-contempt, self-pity; He cannot mean poor-spirited, poor in goods, or "beggars in spirit." Dr. E. Stanley Jones uses the words "renounced in spirit" to give his idea of the meaning. Dr. J. W. G. Ward says:

Christ was constantly using words that had long been in circulation in the realm of religion. This term is one of them. On the lips of the prophets the poor implied not necessarily, or even primarily, those who lacked worldly prosperity. It denoted the godly or the afflicted, the lowly and humble-minded in marked contrast to the self-satisfied, arrogant, proud, and prosperous. And though Luke's account leaves out the phrase "in spirit," to the Jewish mind, the poor stood for those who had come to a just estimate of themselves in the sight of the all-Holy.

Jesus sought to help His apostles see that the ideal man is overwhelmingly aware that he does not have the goods or the attainments for the perfect concept of righteousness as revealed by the Father. He is therefore fully conscious of his imperfections, his lack of that which could measure up in the divine appraisal. He understands that his true wealth depends on something far more precious than anything he might amass. There is a sweet humility of spirit here that has worlds of strength in it. Genuine humility is a badge of greatness, the very threshold to perfect serenity, satisfaction, and sovereignty. This grace is the most perfect instrument to hallow all of life's experiences. The truly humble soul finds himself being released from the temporal and coming into full possession of the eternal.

Peter gives us a beautiful verse: "Be clothed with humility: for God resisteth the proud, but giveth grace to the humble. Humble yourselves therefore under the mighty hand of God, that he may exalt you in due time" (1 Pet. 5:6). How different from the philosophy of Nietzsche: "Assert yourself. Care for nothing except for yourself. The only vice is weakness and the only virtue is strength. Be strong, be a superman. The world is yours if you can get it." In these words is found the abominable cult of self-expression. Jesus came to give life to the deathless philosophy of self-renunciation. Self must be put out completely. Christ must be enthroned as Lord. The fullest and richest blessedness will be ours as we find growing in the garden of our heart that grace of indescribable beauty.

Theirs is the kingdom (3): The Judge who knows the secret excellencies of the deepest heart comes with the supreme gift to the one who is most worthy to receive it and wear it. All the wealth of the divine treasure house is at his disposal. All the riches of divine love and inner heart companionship are his. All that heaven has to offer today and tomorrow are ready for him. It is a beautiful picture.

Blessed are they that mourn (4): We will all agree that mourning is far removed from the desires of men. We do not ask for it as a grace with which to prove our attractiveness. If we regard these words as describing the mourning caused by suffering and sorrow and bereavement, we would still fail to appreciate it as a grace to be desired. It is not beautiful to find one weeping over misspent years. We do not think of congratulating one whose face is wet with tears.

The true man of the kingdom mourns over the sins of the world and over his own lack of that which would please God. In the previous Beatitude we found a humble soul fully aware of his poverty in meeting the demands of God. He is a pauper in such matters. We now find that person weeping and mourning because of that poverty of soul. It is a matter of genuine concern to him. He has found that he has nothing to pay at the gate to life eternal. He is wholly at the mercy of the Father. He can only say, "Nothing in my hand I bring, simply to thy cross I cling."

In addition to his embarrassment because of his own poverty, he has enough of the love of Christ in him to make him weep over the lost condition of others, even as Christ wept over the city of Jerusalem. Blessed is the man who is sensitive to the heart cries of Jerusalem. Blessed is the man who is sensitive to the heart cries of others, even to the darkest heathen land. He loves so much that he mourns and then has an active part in bearing the world's hurt and sin. How beautifully Jesus described Himself! How powerfully He challenges us to be Christlike mourners!

They shall be comforted (4): The word "comfort" is a mighty word. It means much more than solace. It has to do with the giving of powerful inner strength, courage, and "staying" qualities. In Tyndale's translation of Jeremiah 10:4 we find, "They comfort it with nails." Jeremiah was speaking of the process of nailing together bits of wood to fashion a god. The nails were used to give added strength and permanence. Jesus was giving encouragement to the ones who would become the mourners. Inner strength, courage, and perseverance would be given to make the mourner truly "blessed" or "happy" or "to be congratulated." Thanks be unto God for such comfort. It is priceless! It is to be yours! You are to have the measureless resources of the kingdom from which to draw as this prophecy comes true in you. Our Lord wants to give comfort.

Blessed are the meek (5): We have learned to look for delightful surprises as we watch the master Portrait Painter unfold His new facets of beauty and attractiveness. This is his picture of meekness. What is meekness? Is it closely related to humility? It is certainly not to be confused with weakness; there is too much positive strength in it to allow the idea of weakness to stand for a moment. It has a lot to do with self-control. There is poise, balance, and full control of self. There is strength—plenty of it—and so much of it is in reserve that panic and fear are out of the question. Patience has come as a strong ally of all the good reactions of the mind and will.

Moses, Stephen, and the Son of God are the three examples of meekness that stand out before us. They were meek in spirit, strong in will power, gentle in word, poised in decisions, and generous in judgment. Look at our Lord before Pilate. Listen to Him on another occasion when He said, "I came . . . not to do mine own will, but the will of him that sent me" (John 6:38). Again He said, "Learn of me; for I am meek and lowly in heart" (Matt. 11:29). Meekness is a product of the willingness to obey implicitly and to submit to discipline. The kingdom man must have this remarkably valuable quality of soul.

They shall inherit the earth (5): Jesus dared say that the person described in this verse is to come into possession of the earth. Why not? Think back for a moment. Can you think of one more worthy? He is Jesus' choice for that inheritance. Paul said, "All things are yours . . . all are yours; and ye are Christ's" (1 Cor. 3:21–23). The truly humble in heart gains the kingdom of heaven; the mourner gains a precious kingdom of security, strength, and comfort; the meek gain the earth. The Master is telling the truths of the kingdom.

Hunger and thirst after righteousness (6): For what do you hunger and thirst? Be careful of your answer, for it will tell of your inner character, revealing more than you might

imagine. This kingdom man is thoroughly aware of the
value of material possessions, but he finds in himself a longing for something deeper, something more satisfying, something more fully eternal in its significance. It is a sublime
hunger. It is a longing for more than justice—for genuine
goodness of heart, life, and character. It is an intense thirst
for God. The kingdom man longs to be like his Lord in his
inner self. He desires to be right with God and right with
his fellow men. He wants to know the very heart of God.
He seeks to understand the eternal purposes of the Creator
who sent His only begotten Son to die for sinners. He has a
genuine passion for goodness of heart, life, and motive.

They shall be filled (6): How beautiful the promise is!
The fullest satisfaction comes to that man when those holy
longings are fully appraised and satisfied. He will be filled
with blessings; his own heart and life will be infinitely richer,
and people (even to the ends of the earth) will be influenced
for good because of God's matchless gifts to him. What a full
life! Remember that these brief strokes of the brush are
guided by the Son of God, who outlined step by step the
qualities to be found in the man He was choosing to give
the gospel to the whole world. Is He painting your picture?
Does He have full freedom in presenting the lines in your
portrait?

Blessed are the merciful (7): It is fitting that the reference
to "the merciful" should follow immediately upon the word
"righteousness." One who has been feeding upon that rare
food, "righteousness," can be trusted with mercy. Mercy is
really a divine prerogative. It is only as mercy is delegated
by the eternal God that anyone is allowed to give it to others.
It is exceedingly appropriate that this quality is added, since
the righteous person might be cold, unsympathetic, and incapable of the kindness which must characterize the kingdom

man. It is good to have the sweet flavor of mercy mixed with stern righteousness, making the blend so necessary for one who is to carry on for Christ. The good Samaritan is Jesus' example of the merciful man. When the beautiful quality of mercy is in the heart, the outpourings from that heart will be strangely akin to the spirit of Christ. The merciful man is forgiving. Mercy is a quality sorely needed in our world.

He shall obtain mercy (7): It is God who knows how to judge. He renders heavenly mercy to the one who has revealed so much of the spirit of the Master. It was Jesus who said to the frightened sinner, "Neither do I condemn thee." How beautiful to find the emphasis Jesus put on the right sort of inner heart-life. He would have us right toward God and toward men.

Blessed are the pure in heart (8): David had said, "Create in me a clean heart, O God" (Psalm 51:10). Isaiah had written, "Be ye clean, that bear the vessels of the Lord" (52:11). In Proverbs we find, "Keep thy heart with all diligence; for out of it are the issues of life" (4:23). Sir Galahad said, "My strength is as the strength of ten, because my heart is pure." Paul wrote to his young preacher friend, saying, "Keep thyself pure" (1 Tim. 5:22), and a little later to this same young man he said, "If a man shall purge himself from these, he shall be a vessel unto honor, sanctified, fit for the Master's use" (2 Tim. 2:21). John added these words, "Every man who hath this hope in him purifieth himself, even as He is pure" (1 John 3:3).

Jesus demands that the heart, the affections, and the mind be purified as the fountain from which flow the moral and religious life. A pure heart begets a pure life. How priceless are the precious gifts of an unwasted body, soul, and mind! There is a priceless quality, a privilege, a power in purity.

Jesus is describing man's highest possibility, his deepest longings, and his supreme need. Only Christ can make and keep the heart pure.

They shall see God (8): We go back into the meaning of the words "pure in heart" to get a full significance of this prophecy. Only the one who is wholly devoted in heart is allowed to come into the sacred presence of the holy God. There was a man who wanted to see his king. He traveled through several gates up the circular road to the palace. At each gate he was stopped and made to prove that he was completely loyal to the king. Finally, he was admitted to the throne room, since there was no single trace of disloyalty. Only men such as he were allowed to see the face of the king. Jesus said that the pure in heart shall see God. They are the ones admitted to His holy presence.

Blessed are the peacemakers (9): The purity described in the preceding Beatitude is not the kind that builds walls of selfish separation but that which is characterized by action. It is a positive force. Peacemaking is its main job. The kingdom man is lovingly aggressive, doing the very thing that characterizes the Father in heaven. "God was in Christ, reconciling the world unto himself" (2 Cor. 5:19). The kingdom man is challenged by the same kind of inner love for peace and for the souls of others about him. This love becomes his passion, his major business. By his daily impact upon neighbors and friends, he exerts a strong pressure for harmony and peace.

Lincoln's immortal words will always challenge us: "With malice toward none; with charity for all; with firmness in the right, as God gives us to see the right, let us strive on to finish the work we are in; to bind up the nation's wounds; to care for him who shall have borne the battle, and for his widow, and his orphan—to do all which may achieve and cherish a just and lasting peace." In every area of life the ideal man of the kingdom will be working alongside the Prince of peace. Making peace is Christ's highest and best work. In that task we follow Him joyously.

They shall be called sons of God (9): This phrase refers to the name given peacemakers by neighbors, friends, and associates. They have already been called children by the Father. They have exerted such a beautiful influence day by day that they have established themselves as related to God in character and activity. They sow and cultivate the flowers of the Spirit in their garden. They drive out enmity, envy, suspicion, misunderstanding, and discord. Their text is, "Be ye reconciled to God." They are actively devoted to the holy task of bringing peace into hearts, homes, and nations.

Blessed are the persecuted (10–12): If we are sure that we have not deserved persecution, we may claim it as a prize to be enjoyed. The exceptionally aggressive spirit called "the peacemaker" will almost inevitably stir up some opposition, resentment, and criticism. Someone will resent his efforts, and the world will "kick back" in persecution. The person who is able to stand through the storm and continue his unselfish work of reconciliation is singled out for strong commendation by our Lord. How comforting it is to know that the Master knows and understands and calls him "blessed." Many have qualified through the years since Jesus' words were spoken and have found a rich inner experience as the Saviour's strong arm has been about them.

Rejoice and be exceeding glad (12): Out of the midst of hostility, criticism, and reviling, the ideal man will manifest a joyful spirit which will amaze those who see the beauty of his spirit. Such a spirit is so rare, so beautiful, so like the Master that worldly minds have difficulty understanding it.

It has always been so. The prophets, the saints of God, the martyrs, and the faithful pastors who have continued daily in the triumphant witness to the fact of the presence of Christ in the heart have found genuine joy in being given grace to carry on for Him. The *reward in heaven* is rich, but the actual reward that comes day by day is too rich for mere words to describe. The most beautiful living in the world is the sweet Christlike living exhibited by saints who are persecuted falsely for His sake. Thank God for the kind of spirit within that fits true Christians for that brand of living.

If you would know how to acquire and enjoy the qualities revealed by our Lord in these Beatitudes, you may find some of the secrets in 1 Cor. 13:4–7, Gal. 5:22–23, and 1 Cor. 6:19. He wants us to measure up to this portrait. The Holy Spirit stands ready to make victorious living possible. He would have us catch step with Him and move out in devoted living.

THE INFLUENCE OF KINGDOM MEN (13–16)

We have followed the Teacher as He has painted the colorful portrait of the true disciple. He has emphasized what the disciple is on the inside; his character stands out before us. The Teacher is now ready to tell us of that man's influence in the world about him. Privilege always entails responsibility. The man is to make an impact on his world. The character developed according to Jesus' pattern has the definite responsibility of exerting positive influence on the world. Jesus dared look upon a group of peasants from Galilee and Judea and declare to them that He was depending on them to be "the hope of the world." They must save the world from moral decay and moral darkness. How could these obscure men become so powerful and valuable that Jesus could lay the promotion of the gospel upon their shoulders? Obligations and responsibilities mingle with privileges. This is the Master's way.

Ye are the salt of the earth (13): There is corruption, decay, and rottenness in the world about us. The kingdom man is set down near those whose lives are corrupt to bring health and soundness to the community and to individuals.

Salt saves from putrefaction, and it saves from insipidity. Salt is aseptic. It prevents the spread of corruption. Jesus makes His pertinent point that our world needs those who are "the salt of the earth" in the spots where their presence will powerfully affect the very atmosphere about them. Their homes, their neighborhoods, and their world will be strangely better because of the effect that they exert on the spirit and life of the neighbors and people. Christian character is a positive force in the world. Its witness is to be powerful, pungent, purposeful, public, and prayerful. Dare to be different for Christ's sake. He counts on you.

How pathetic the words, *But if the salt have lost its savour, wherewith shall it be salted . . . good for nothing . . . cast out . . . under foot of men* (5:13). The salt in Palestine could, and did, lose its savor. It was useless. How much more tragic is the Christian who has become *good for nothing!* Can that be Christ's appraisal of you? What sort of salt are you?

Ye are the light of the world (14): This picture is even more daring—more thrilling. The Master is counting on us to turn our faces to Him so that His light will strike our faces and be reflected into every dark corner of the globe. He declared that *a city set on a hill cannot be hid.* It was said of Jesus, "He could not be hid" (Mark 7:24). It is impossible for the kingdom man to fail in his task of giving light when he maintains the radiance that comes from our dear Lord. Jesus said of Himself, "I am the light of the world: he that followeth me shall not walk in darkness, but shall have the light of life" (John 8:12).

Do you complain that your lot is set in the midst of darkness, squalor, and sin? Why not? You are *light*—exactly what that spot needs. Imagine a lighthouse complaining that it is doomed to stand on a danger point in the dense darkness. Where else would it want to stand? Listen to Paul as he talks to his friends at Philippi: "In the midst of a crooked and perverse generation . . . ye shine as lights (lighthouses) in the world; holding forth the word of life" (Phil. 2:15–16) .

That light is *set on a hill* and that lamp *in the house.* Your light is to shine in the quiet of the home circle so that the family group need not walk in darkness. It is also to be set on a hill so that it may reach farther and influence the people round about. Your light is to extend to the last boundary, too, because you are "the light of the world."

What a joy it is to know that every line of these words in Matthew 5 is related to us and directed to us. We are His chosen ones. He has plans for reaching the whole world that include us and our ministry. He has redeemed us, saved us, chosen us, and empowered us in order that we might do His bidding and bring the lost ones of the world to Him. May all His rich grace be powerfully moved forward to them through us as willing instruments until they shall all know Him, love Him, and follow Him.

We would not, we pray, hide our lights. We would not let sin and its darkness dim the splendor of the grace of God as it would shine through us. As the wick must be kept trimmed and the lamp clean, so must our lives be kept disciplined and pure. Nor would we allow the weakening power of sin to dilute the salt of our lives so that they, like worthless salt, be valuable only as footpaths. Claiming the power of the One who has given us our task, we would dedicate our lives to lighting and seasoning the world in which we live.

When we have let our lights shine and ourselves be used for seasoning and healing the world, we can also expect the greatest gift the Father has for His children: we shall be "blessed."

Ye are salt . . . ye are light.

Isaiah LIII

He shall grow up before him as a tender plant, as a root out of a dry ground. . . . He is despised and rejected of men; . . . he was despised, and we esteemed him not. . . .

We did esteem him stricken, smitten of God, and afflicted. But he was wounded for our transgressions, he was bruised for our iniquities: the chastisement of our peace was upon him; and with his stripes we are healed. All we like sheep have gone astray; we have turned every one to his own way; and the Lord hath laid on him the iniquity of us all.

He was oppressed . . . afflicted, yet he opened not his mouth: he is brought as a lamb to the slaughter, and as a sheep before her shearers is dumb, so he openeth not his mouth. . . . He was cut off out of the land of the living: for the transgression of my people was he stricken. And he made his grave with the wicked, and with the rich in his death; because he had done no violence, neither was any deceit in his mouth.

Yet it pleased the Lord to bruise him; . . . the pleasure of the Lord shall prosper in his hand. He shall see of the travail of his soul, and shall be satisfied . . . because he hath poured out his soul unto death: and he was numbered with the transgressors; and he bare the sin of many, and made intercession for the transgressors.

VI. Foregleams of Calvary

_____*Isaiah LIII*

WERE YOU THERE when they crucified my Lord?" You were not there. You will always be dependent on the report of one who can describe the scene in detail. You would naturally turn to the Four Gospels for the clearest account of that never-to-be-forgotten experience. Did it ever occur to you to go to Isaiah for the most unusual, the most exciting, and the most gripping description of that scene? You will find that this chapter is the keenest interpretation of the events in that dramatic moment in the history of redemption. This chapter sounds more like a New Testament evangelist than an Old Testament prophet. The writer stood centuries ahead on the hilltop outside the city wall and watched each movement. Then he gave an accurate interpretation of what happened.

This section is the last of the four Servant poems (42:1–8; 49:1–7; 50:4–9; 52:13–53:12). The Messiah has been pictured in each of them. As Teacher, Prophet, and Evangelist, He walks before us. In this poem He appears as the Suffering Servant, the martyr Prophet, the Sin-bearer. This chapter is the "Mount Everest" of Old Testament prophecy. It is the psalm of the Sufferer.

The fifteen verses (beginning with 52:13 and continuing through 53:12) are divided into five stanzas of three verses each. The first strophe has nine lines, the second has ten, the third has eleven, the fourth has thirteen, and the fifth has fourteen. The great truths seem to gather added richness and press forward with ever-increasing fulness to the final syllable. God's glorious message of comfort reaches its climax in this messianic hymn of suffering, expiation, death, and triumph. The writing is unbelievably superb in every detail.

THE FIRST STROPHE (52:13–15)

The Servant is presented dramatically as the favorite of the Father. Announcement is made that He is to work His way, wisely, prudently, and successfully to a victorious completion of the redemptive plan of God. The highest exaltation is to be His in the ages to come, an eternally precious reward for His sacrifice. Present degradation is contrasted with future glory.

The Hebrew word *hiskil* presents the idea of having insight, dealing prudently, and pressing forward to the full completion of the purpose of God. Thus the translation, "deal wisely," and the rendering, "shall prosper," both carry a part of the meaning. Both ideas in the translation make it complete. The Servant has keen insight, acts prudently in every moment of the terrible ordeal, and completes the full redemptive purpose of the Father by His persistent pressing forward with the divine blueprint before Him. His suffering is fruitful. It ends in glory. Through humiliation He comes to the highest exaltation. He knows what He is doing, where He is going, why this thing must be done, and what He can expect at the end of the bitter humiliation. The exaltation will come.

These words—*exalted, lifted up,* and *very high*—present a picture of rising into view, being lifted to a higher place and then standing triumphantly on the height. Some interpreters go so far as to let these words predict the resurrection, the ascension, and the place on high with the Father.

In verses fourteen and fifteen the Servant is addressed. The word *shamem* (astonied) expresses the people's utter amazement at the sight that greets them. They are completely bewildered and petrified. The Servant's unparalleled sufferings are too much for them. The stretched and quivering body on the tree, the gashed and bloody face under a crown of cruel thorns, the bleeding back, the unbelievable shame, the spectacle of the sufferer in the midst of "howling wolves," and the gruesome sight of death renders them helpless as they watch. He is pictured as a sufferer in the agony of death throes too disfigured to be recognized, too pathetic to be attractive, too deep in humiliation and shame to be chosen.

The verb *hizzah,* sometimes translated "sprinkle," does not mean that here. The literal meaning of the word is to "spring" or "leap." The causative indicates (as here) a sudden movement of astonishment in startled amazement. The people tremble in astonishment as they look upon such breath-taking deeds.

Kings shut their mouths as they look on Him. Slowly it dawns on them that the cruel suffering being endured before their eyes is revealing One who is to be highly exalted and have a place in God's plan, One who is to be covered with glory and honor. They are struck dumb as they see the heights to which the Sufferer is to come. The way to sovereignty is the way of suffering.

The inspired author put down in the first stanza his introduction, acquainting us with the theme of the poem. He sums up the thought in the announcement that the Servant is to be highly exalted after the severest and most humiliating sufferings ever witnessed. Travail issues in triumph. Pain leads to glory.

THE SECOND STROPHE (53:1-3)

Look upon the features of that wonderful portrait. Watch His eventful career unfold. The Servant is under the watchful eye of God and the eyes of men. The prophet, speaking for his people, confesses the tragic error they have made. They were all wrong in their conclusions about the Servant. They had thought of Him as one wholly unworthy of consideration.

A literal translation of verse one would be, "Who could have believed that which was announced to us, and the arm of Jehovah, on whom was it disclosed? The report which reached our ears was so incredible that no one of us was prepared to take it in." Only one prepared in heart by the Holy Spirit could see, understand, and believe such a report. Uninitiated minds could not be expected to accept it. How could one come to think of a divine Redeemer in terms of debasing humiliation and excruciating suffering? No one wants to think of a conquering Representative from the throne of heaven making His way through labyrinths of shame, rejection, suffering, and death. Nothing about this way to triumph and sovereignty fits into the picture usually envisioned.

The arm of the Lord is a biblical symbol for the unleashed power of Jehovah for a specific purpose and at a given moment. That arm was revealed in creation (John 1:3), in the incarnation (John 1:14), and in Jehovah's eternal rule from the heavenly throne (Rev. 4:1-11). This note gives notice of the symbol's true fulfilment in the person and miraculous work of the Son of God, for in the Son the "arm of the Lord" is truly revealed. He is the volunteer to carry out the divine purpose to redeem fallen men everywhere. The full power of Jehovah was ever resident in Him, even though blind eyes and stupid minds were incapable of sensing the wonder and glory of His presence.

He grew up: The prophet seeks to explain why the Servant was not accepted and idolized. In order to give us the whole story, he goes back to Jesus' childhood. He explains that to worldly minds there was nothing to commend the young lad as the divine Messiah. No one who saw Him would guess the secret. His contemporaries were poorly prepared to understand Him; they failed utterly to suspect Him of a heavenly commission.

He grew up before him: Under Jehovah's watchful eye the Servant grew to manhood. Men did not know. Even the members of His family and the religious leaders of His day did not suspect that He was growing daily in the sight of the Father. Listen to the attestations of Jehovah's loving care at Jesus' baptism (Matt. 3:17), on the Mount of Transfiguration (Matt. 17:5), and in the eventful hour when the Greeks came asking for Jesus (John 12:28). All His life before His incarnation and all His life as a human being were constantly under the watchful eye of the Father in heaven.

As seen by men: What was the human view? He grew up before the people of His generation. They were blind to beauty. They had very poor faculties for judging true worth. They had worldly ideas and superficial conceptions of how a Messiah should look and behave. The author confesses that they erred altogether in judging the One who grew up before them.

They saw Him as a "sapling," a "tender plant," a "delicate twig" or "sucker" growing out from the trunk or stump of an old tree. They saw Him as a *root out of dry ground,* lying on the dry, hard pathway, spurned and kicked away by careless feet. How could anyone think appreciatively of one so observed and treated? How could anyone regard Him as possessing qualities that might produce fruit? To these men, thinking in terms of military might, pomp, and splendor, the Messiah made no impression whatever. He did not "look the part." "Comeliness" is equivalent to "majesty" or "splendor" or "showy" attractiveness.

When they compared Him with their false conceptions of the Messiah, they were not disposed to look the second time. Add to these negative concepts the positive elements of suffering and agony and shame, and the problem becomes more difficult. In their thinking, ugly sins lay behind bodily sufferings. Who would want to choose one with these characteristics as a kingly conqueror?

Despised, forsaken: As a result of His cruel persecution, His tragic sufferings, and His shame and humiliation on the cross, men of worldly conceptions turned away in horror and disgust. "They reckoned him not," or "held him of no account." Men hid their faces and walked away from Him. What a commentary on man's distorted understanding of spiritual matters! How pathetic to see God's beloved Messiah walking among the men He came to redeem without any power to make them pause and recognize Him and welcome Him as Redeemer! The great ones kept aloof from Him. The religious leaders, who treasured the Scriptures, refused to recognize Him and turned away in disgust. They could not see in Him the qualities they attributed to the Messiah. He continued on, *despised, forsaken, rejected.* He was entirely alone.

THE THIRD STROPHE (4–6)

Those who rejected, forsook, and misunderstood the Messiah now confess that they were completely mistaken about Him and His sufferings. They had followed the reasoning of Job's friends and had come to the conclusion that He was a great sinner, feeling the punishing strokes of the divine hand for His own sins. His sufferings marked Him as one on whom God rained full punishment. The author reverses this verdict completely and, in confessing to us their error, reveals the true meaning of substitution. They saw His suffering. They learned that He was innocent. They came to see that His suffering was vicarious. He was the divinely chosen substitute. His sacrifice was not only vicarious but redemptive. It was effective. Victory was assured.

Note the dominant notes of this stanza and the expressions for suffering: *griefs, sorrows, wounded, bruised, smitten, chastisement, stripes*. Note the vivid use of "our" and "he." *Saval*—borne—describes the toilsome carrying of a heavy burden one has chosen for his own back. *Nasa*—carried—signifies taking the guilt on himself as his own and carrying it, paying the penalty of it. The author realizes that the Messiah has done just this for the sinning people.

These people had seen Him as a *nagu'a,* one stricken with some horrible disease, penalty, or divine curse. In addition to this, He was *mukkeh,* smitten of God, and then *me'unneh,* humbled or loaded down with crushing sufferings. These words sum up their conclusions concerning the meaning of His pain and suffering. They realize that they were wrong. His suffering was from God. Sin caused it. But one "detail" made worlds of difference. The Messiah was not the sinner. He was bearing the sin for the sinners. He was accepting the heavy stroke for them.

He was pierced: The verb *halal* describes a heart wounded unto death but still alive. We would say "mortally wounded." In this verse we have a passive form that is best translated "pierced through." No stronger word could be used. It was a mortal wound He sustained.

Crushed: Medukka indicates complete and nearly fatal injuries inflicted purposely and maliciously. The damage was serious. The translation "bruised" is hardly enough to carry the full weight of this word.

For our transgressions: The author makes it perfectly clear that he has come to know that the Messiah did not suffer for His own sins but for the sins of those about Him. Death, following agonizing suffering, was the penalty. The Messiah gladly and willingly paid the full price. Atonement was effected. Wounded, pierced through, crushed, beaten— He took it all. He is the only victim; He is a voluntary victim; He is a vicarious victim; He is a victorious victim.

Chastisement leading to our peace: The word "chastisement" signifies a particular punishment which came upon the Servant by God's appointment. The word sums up all the various aspects of pain, suffering, shame, and punishment that came upon the Messiah in the bitter experience on Golgotha. All that it took to purchase full peace for every soul was included in this line that tells of the hours of agony. Peace is expensive. What a price He had to pay to secure it!

His stripes . . . healed: The people were sick unto death because of their sins. They could not heal themselves. They were in desperate straits. The Servant took upon Himself a suffering unto death that healing might come to them. His voluntary submission to endure the stripes, or weals, made that healing at once effective. He endured the curse, submitted to the chastisement, and took the painful stripes to procure full soul healing for them.

Had gone . . . had turned: Selfishness caused all this suffering. Heedlessly and selfishly the people had turned into the way that seemed desirable. It has always been so. Selfish gratification has dictated the behavior of men and women since the earliest beginnings in the garden of Eden. Free choice has been a divinely given privilege, but it has allowed a freedom that has proved exceedingly costly to men of all ages. Wrecks on the road, ugly failures, sinful indulgences, disgraceful influence, and divine heartaches have come in the wake of God's gift of choice.

Made to light on him: Strangely enough, these men who so wilfully went their own way in sin and rebellion did not have to bear the cruel blow of punishment. It fell on the innocent person of the Messiah. The Lord Jehovah caused to light on Him the guilt of all men. The guilt that was ours concentrated upon Him. Just as a certain glass will collect and concentrate the rays from the sun and center them upon a given spot, so the guilt from all the world was put upon Him. The wrath of God was concentrated in the same fashion and found its mark for utter destruction. It was our sin that the Son bore. It was our salvation He suffered to procure. Our redemption was purchased when He went to the cross for us.

The Servant's sole form of service has thus been pictured for us in this immortal poem. His work was not to be the Teacher, the Example, the Benefactor, the Reformer. His one eternal work was to be bruised for our iniquities that we might be redeemed through faith in Him. Though writing many hundred years before the crucifixion of our Lord, the author has accurately and vividly portrayed the succession of events and has interpreted it better than any contemporary theologian could have done. The Holy Spirit revealed more than the author knew. Except for the Holy Spirit's inspiration, this poem could not have been written.

THE FOURTH STROPHE (7–9)

In this lovely stanza we see the atoning Lamb at work making full atonement for our sins. The Messiah suffers, dies, and is buried. His sweet demeanor, under His undeserved sufferings, calls forth our admiration as we begin to see the richer and deeper meanings of His sacrificial death.

He was oppressed—abused—tortured. Cruel torture was meted out because of erroneous judgments of Him. How cruel it all was! How utterly inhuman and barbarous! How could human beings resort to such indignities, abuses, and outrageous deeds as these? They were blind, prejudiced, ignorant, and strangely lacking in ordinary decency. *Yet he humbled himself.* "Humbled" stands in striking contrast to "oppressed." We are dealing with One who saw clearly the goal of all the suffering. His spirit was right. He understood the blindness, the prejudice, the ignorance, the cruelty, and the inhuman treatment. He suffered willingly! Here is the key to the whole matter. His endurance was unremonstrating and unresisting.

A lamb . . . led to the slaughter: His quiet submissiveness has been the marvel of the ages. *He opened not his mouth.* Not a protest, not a complaint, not a murmur passed his lips. He is called the Lamb of God. He is pictured as the perfect example of the perfect sacrifice. He revealed the true spirit of the world's Redeemer. Why should He protest? Why should He be noisy, loud, and rebellious? He was as truly "about his Father's business" at that moment as at any other moment in all eternity. The pain, agony, and suffering

were tragically excruciating. The sin caused to light on Him
was unspeakably revolting. It caused His righteous soul to
recoil in horror. But the Lamb of God moved on to make
atonement for sin. He willingly accepted all the horrible
features of the experience of Golgotha because He loved the
Father and loved to do His will, because He loved sinful men
and would be their Redeemer and Saviour. He said, "I lay
down my life for the sheep . . . No one taketh it from me,
but I lay it down of myself. I have power to lay it down,
and I have power to take it again" (John 10:17–18). He was
a voluntary victim. He was the personal Sufferer, the vicarious Sufferer, the silent Sufferer. He was in perfect agreement with God.

John the Baptist spoke of Christ as the Lamb of God taking away the sin of the world. Peter quoted this very prophecy: "Knowing that ye were redeemed . . . with the precious blood of Christ, as of a lamb without blemish and without spot, even the blood of Christ" (1 Pet. 1:18–19). In the
Apocalypse Christ is often designated as the Lamb of God
(Rev. 7:10, 17; 12:10–11; 14:4; 21:23, 27).

By tyranny and by judgment he was taken: The Servant's
death was a hurried and precipitous thing accomplished by
human hands and human law. In fact, it was a judicial murder. Those who killed him were working under God's plan,
but their thoughts and their designs and their movements
were dominated by hatred, and their execution of an evil
plot was utterly selfish. Their plan did serve to release Him
from His sufferings and permit Him to carry out His purpose to die as Redeemer.

He was cut off . . . he was stricken unto death: Murder
is clearly charged. Again let us realize that the tragic means
used to end His life were but instruments in the divine
hand to make the atonement possible. The author is certain

that it was "for the transgression of my people" that the stroke came upon Him. We cannot get far without being reminded of the substitutionary teaching that lies at the bottom of the doctrine so clearly enunciated here. Sin brought the stroke of death upon the innocent head of the Messiah.

His grave . . . his death: Even in death the unjust treatment continued and the hatred of enemies did not stop. But for the kindly intervention of Joseph of Arimathea the grave of our Lord might have been among the common criminals in the despised area of the city. In His death He was hanged between two felons who were being executed for their crimes. In His burial the loving hands of Joseph and Nicodemus gave all that riches and love could provide.

He had done no violence: All these indignities seem to be pathetically out of place since the Servant was sinless in heart and character. Innocence shines forth as a beautiful mark of His inner nature. In spite of His sinless life these deeds of violence and these spiteful indignities came upon Him.

Dead and buried! Was that the end? *Cut off . . . taken . . . stricken!* How about the future? He was innocent, sinless, the beloved of the Father, and yet the dire calamity fell upon Him.

THE FIFTH STROPHE (10–12)

The real purpose of the sufferings of the Messiah will be clear as we see God's plan for the salvation of the people of the earth. The Servant is to be God's special instrument in establishing His kingdom through His work in removing guilt and bringing multitudes to righteousness. Even though cut off out of the land of the living, He will come back in triumph to use His power to produce spiritual sons and daughters and to make possible a world turning to Him.

The resurrection of the Servant is clearly pictured and affirmed.

Yet it pleased . . . to bruise: Again we are brought face to face with the fact that while men inflicted the wounds and caused the Servant's death, it was Jehovah who actually decreed them. His holy will was carried out by men. The word "pleased" seems a bit out of place in the light of the present use of that English word. Divine love was strong, but even in His love for His Son the Father was able to find unusual satisfaction in seeing the atonement brought about. Only by crushing, piercing, and wounding the Servant could sin be blotted out and redemption accomplished. The Father was pleased when He looked beyond the person of His Son and saw the redeemed ones of all the earth receiving salvation.

His soul an offering for sin: No other offering could effect salvation. No other means could be found to save men. God the Father made the soul of His Son a guilt offering, and the Son willingly became that guilt offering to give full salvation to anyone down through the ages who might come to Him in simple trust. He would pay the full price once and for all that full redemption might be secured. God willed it. The Servant did it. The eternal victory was complete. To the end of time men and women can come claiming that precious redemption.

He shall see his seed . . . shall prolong his days: In verse eight there is the sad news that the Servant's sudden and untimely death ended any hope of sons and daughters. Now we are assured that His atoning sacrifice will make it possible for uncounted multitudes to be His children. (Cf. Rev. 7:9, "A great multitude no man can number," and Heb. 2:10, "In bringing many sons to glory.") He was violently cut off and yet "He shall prolong His days." By His resurrection

He is not only to live again but is to have power to multiply those days beyond measure.

The purpose of Jehovah shall prosper: We have been assured that the Servant is to see that the universal religion shall be set up and that it is to prosper. Now the outcome is even clearer since the death of the Servant accomplished the great victory. There is to be victory ahead. God's great purpose is to be signally realized.

He shall see of the travail of his soul and be satisfied: On Golgotha the Messiah saw the travail of His soul. That travail was seen in the pain in hands and feet and back, in the rejection of those to whom He came, in the taunts and jeers and insults of those about Him, in the full realization of the Father's blazing wrath at human sin, in the agony of being touched by sin, in the fury of hell's torture as He carried your sins and mine until all of them were literally consumed, and in the death throes as "He poured out his soul unto death."

He shall be satisfied: Here is another beautiful mystery, radiant with the glory of eternal grace. We read, "It pleased Jehovah to crush him." We now hear that "He shall be satisfied." In what could the Messiah find satisfaction? He would be exceedingly happy when He saw the full glory that would come to the Father. He would rejoice when He saw the uncounted millions coming in sincere faith to become new creatures. How happy He could become as He looked upon uncounted "trophies of grace." He would shout for joy as He recognized the beautiful character produced in His own followers. He would find peculiar joy in watching the complete destruction of the devil and his entire kingdom. We do not wonder that He is "satisfied."

The eternal Servant, who suffered, was rejected, killed, buried, and rose again, now lives victoriously, making intercession and rejoicing as countless multitudes come to Him. He has earned the right to "make many righteous" and to receive the plaudits of the redeemed. *He poured out his soul unto death.* His vicarious death made life eternal possible for all men everywhere. Faith in Him brings salvation.

SUMMARY

Paul says, "God was in Christ, reconciling the world unto Himself" (2 Cor. 5:19). This matchless poem tells us of our sin, of Christ's substitution, of His sufferings, of God's satisfaction, and of the eternal victory possible because of Christ's death on the cross. As long as time lasts, the message of the cross will challenge the best thinking of men everywhere. The Son's love led Him to suffer and die. His love still calls to us to fall at His feet and let His healing touch bring the fullest life and the surest salvation.

> When I survey the wondrous cross,
> On which the Prince of glory died,
> My richest gain I count but loss,
> And pour contempt on all my pride.
>
> Forbid it, Lord, that I should boast,
> Save in the death of Christ my God;
> All the vain things that charm me most,
> I sacrifice them to His blood.
>
> See, from His head, His hands, His feet,
> Sorrow and love flow mingled down;
> Did e'er such love and sorrow meet,
> Or thorns compose so rich a crown.
>
> Were the whole realm of nature mine,
> That were a present far too small;
> Love so amazing, so divine,
> Demands my soul, my life, my all.
>
> ISAAC WATTS

Luke XV

A certain man had two sons: and the younger of them said to his father, Father, give me the portion of goods that falleth to me. And he divided unto them his living. And not many days after the younger son gathered all together, and took his journey into a far country, and there wasted his substance with riotous living. And when he had spent all, there arose a mighty famine in that land; and he began to be in want. And he went and joined himself to a citizen of that country; and he sent him into his field to feed swine. And he would fain have filled his belly with the husks that the swine did eat: and no man gave to him.

And when he came to himself, he said, How many hired servants of my father's have bread enough and to spare, and I perish with hunger! I will arise and go to my father. . . . And he arose, and came to his father. But when he was yet a great way off, his father saw him, and had compassion, and ran, and fell on his neck, and kissed him. And the son said unto him, Father, I have sinned . . . and am no more worthy to be called thy son. But the father said, . . . Bring forth the best robe . . . a ring . . . shoes . . . the fatted calf. . . . And they began to be merry.

VII. The Love of God

_____Luke XV

IN THIS PASSAGE of exquisite beauty, Jesus presents the love of God in all of its tenderness and plaintive appeal. When you have looked at each line of it, you are overwhelmed by the sheer sweetness of the Father's inexhaustible love for lost men and women. You reach the place where you are not concerned with how the person looks or how well-to-do he is or what rung of the social ladder he is on. The fact that he is lost moves you, and you find your heart going out to him immediately. You have a powerful urge to help him find salvation through Christ. This chapter is one of the tallest peaks in the whole range of Scripture mountains.

In it God stands out as being infinitely concerned about every man. He recognizes the peril of the lost person and is moved with compassion for him. He knows how utterly helpless the sinner is. He will not be satisfied until warning, seeking, finding, pleading, and bringing have all done their part in making salvation an accomplished fact in the sinner's life. Jesus reveals the true heart of God. We will know Him better when we have looked closely at this picture.

THE OCCASION (1–2)

Jesus was nearing the end of His earthly ministry. Only a
few days remained before the trials and. the crucifixion. For
days great crowds had followed him, listening intently to
His penetrating messages. He was making the terms of dis-
cipleship so high that great concern was felt. How could
anyone become His disciple? How would anyone dare reach
up to meet His high demands? Closest to Him were to be
found the publicans and sinners. Surely these despised and
hated people needed. the gospel. Could they become disciples? Jesus was moved with compassion and greatly stirred
in soul as He turned to them with a warmth and a welcome
that was born of His sincere love. He was happy to explain
the way of salvation to them and to assure them that the
love of God included them. He had said, "The Son of man
is come to seek and to save that which was lost" (Luke 19:10).
He was ready to prove it.

There were other interested listeners. The leaders of the
Jewish religious life were busy watching, listening, and making an ugly uproar. What had Jesus done? They had seen
Him show concern for the worst sinners in the town. They
said, "This man receiveth sinners" (15:2). These unwashed
sinners were not worthy to have even a glance of interest
turned their way. They were to be despised, scorned,
spurned, and pushed aside like so many undesirable bits of
trash. These leaders had an ugly spirit. It must have cast
quite a chill over the sensitive soul of the Lord Jesus. They
were not even slightly concerned about the salvation of such
low creatures.

Under the pressure of this selfish spirit, Jesus gave us this
marvelous parable. We deplore such behavior, but we are
indebted to the embarrassing situation that brought forth

Jesus' most beautiful parable. It will always be a treasure for all those who would know how the Father loves and how the vilest sinner may receive salvation. As the parable unfolded, perhaps the Pharisees and the scribes saw God's estimate of them as well as His love for all sinners everywhere. They were included in the plan of God to save the world. They needed the salvation Christ came to purchase. They could find soul satisfaction in precisely the same way as these publicans could. They would be welcomed as heartily and cleansed by the same blood. They would then be fit to go to other sinners with the gospel message.

THE PARABLE (3–32)

Jesus addressed the parable (really three parables) to His cynical critics. These self-righteous religious leaders needed a sermon. They lacked compassion for the lost. They were not willing to see sinners come to God for salvation. They would keep salvation for themselves.

Jesus spoke to them of a shepherd seeking his sheep that was lost, of a woman searching diligently for a silver coin that was lost, and of a father who waited at the front gate for a wayward son who was lost in a far country. His parables about the lost sheep, the lost coin, and the lost boy were designed to explain, illustrate, and defend His concern for lost men and His joy in receiving them. They were true and vivid pictures of God's compassion for every life that is lost.

Some of the lost are like stupid sheep that have wandered aimlessly out into the wilderness where they are incapable of finding their way back to the fold. Some are lost like a coin dropped accidentally by one who should have been more careful. Some are lost like the wilful boy who left his father's home and made his way deliberately to the far country. In each case the owner was greatly concerned. In each case there was much rejoicing when the lost one was safe at home again.

Henry Burton Farrar reminds us that this parable (3–32) gives us pictures of the bewildered sinner (3–7), the unconscious sinner (8–10), and the voluntary sinner (11–32). He might have added a fourth picture, that of the ugliest sinner (25–32).

We are face to face with a song concerning the grace of God. The Father had plenty for all men everywhere. The Saviour was happy to tell of it and describe its miraculous work in the hearts of sinners. Publicans and sinners need not draw back. The grace of God was for them. It would bring eternal salvation through faith. Christ died to save them and wanted them to come to Him and find that salvation for themselves.

THE SHEPHERD AND THE SHEEP (4–7)

Here is a heart-stirring picture. The Good Shepherd loves, seeks, suffers, finds, and brings the sheep home. He rejoices. The shepherd in the parable did each of these things. The sheep had wandered away and was lost. The shepherd went for him. It was a difficult journey. The search called for much effort, but the shepherd was overjoyed when he found his sheep. He took him on his own shoulder and brought him home. He called out for all his neighbors to rejoice with him.

How like the Good Shepherd! Jesus was describing Himself! He was showing the divine estimate of a human soul. He was giving a glimpse of the great heart of the Father. He was drawing a picture of poor, stupid, deluded, wandering man, utterly helpless in the grip of sin's wilderness. The Shepherd must go in tenderness and love to find him and bring him home. Redeemed men who know the way home are urged to go and find the lost one and bring him to the Saviour for healing. How thrilling it is to have the curtain pulled aside for a moment that we may see and hear the shouts of rejoicing because one lost one has been brought home. The Master would have you and me help in this sacred work.

THE SILVER COIN (8–10)

The woman possessed ten lovely silver coins. She treasured them. They represented the total amount of her wealth. Perhaps they were the sacred string of small coins given to her by her husband as a betrothal gift. Nothing could be more precious to her. One of them slipped off and rolled away across the room to some dark spot where it was completely hidden. She was greatly disturbed. Her treasure was gone. She must find it. She lighted a lamp, got a broom, and went to work, frantically searching for the little piece of money. The search was thorough, careful, persevering, and unceasing. It was successful. How happy she was to have the coin in her trembling hand again! Immediately she called in neighbors and friends to rejoice with her. She had found her precious coin.

Jesus was teaching the same lesson. The lost person represented by the coin is not at all conscious of his lost condition nor of his real worth to the loving Father. But he is still God's creature and actually carries the image of the king stamped upon him. He is capable of restoration, but God alone can restore him. The Holy Spirit goes in diligent search until he is found. Every soul is recoverable, and God does not will that one of them shall continue being lost. Even the angels join in the rejoicing when the lost one is brought home. Jesus sought every opportunity to reveal to His critics the welcome that awaits a sinner who is saved.

THE FATHER AND THE PRODIGAL (11–32)

Ernest Fremont Tittle says, "No story ever told has less need of interpretation than this matchless parable of human folly and divine love. God's concern for the 'lost' is here set forth in terms at once completely simple and profoundly moving." [1] How right he is! The story is a matchless bit of artistry, too intricately beautiful to be ruined by too much dissecting. It has been called "the crown and pearl of all." The glad tidings of the full, free, life-giving gospel are clearly presented. God is pictured as always willing to receive wayward, wilful, wandering sinners who have lost their outward attractiveness if they will come in their rags and starved condition with confession and genuine repentance. Arms of mercy will always reach out to such sinners to pull them to the loving heart of God.

We are conscious of a clearer picture of the sinner, too. He comes before us as a selfish, headstrong, restless prodigal who chose to claim his inheritance and get completely away from the restraining influence of his father. With reckless abandon he literally threw his possessions away in dissolute living. Disaster, want, misery, and hunger drove him deeper into the godless life. Coming to himself, he went speedily to his father's house. His spirit of repentance, confession, and humility commend him to us.

THE FATHER OF THE PRODIGAL

The father provided all for the boy. Behind all other considerations we are made conscious of the fact that the father

---

[1] *The Gospel According to Luke* (New York: Harper & Brothers Publishers, 1951), p. 168.

was the great provider. The father of the boy had produced all the goods, all the comforts, all the estate for his boy. The Heavenly Father made all the blessings that each human being enjoys. How great is our debt to Him!

The father also loved the boy and wanted him near. We may be sure that the father in the story had great plans for years of happiness, fellowship, and enjoyable work with his two boys. We know that the divine Creator has so much love for His creatures that He wants them near Him and in fellowship with Him. We can never know how much He loves us. We can never fathom the deep purpose of God that includes each one of God's redeemed sons. We can only rejoice that it is so.

The father allowed free choice. Even though sorrow filled his heart, the earthly father readily gave the son the privilege of exercising free choice. The Heavenly Father allows free choice to an almost unbelievable degree. It is at once the most precious and the most dangerous possession the young prodigal can possess. A mere human being with little intelligence, little judgment, little experience, and little thought of the effect of his actions on others or the effect on the Kingdom is allowed to exercise his privilege of choice and make a sudden decision that may be disastrous. It may make him or wreck him. It may bring heartache and suffering to others. The will of the loving Father in heaven is that each of us shall have that special endowment from heaven's throne. How marvelous and yet how hazardous!

The father suffered while the boy squandered all. It is easy to think of the miseries, the privation, and the sufferings of the boy during those days in the far country, but we do not usually pause to think of the acute sufferings of the father. There is disappointment, fear, loneliness, and hunger in the heart of a father who continues to wait for the return of a wayward child. If that is true of the earthly father of the prodigal, how much more acute and dreadful is the suffering of the Heavenly Father, who sees and understands and knows all that is in the boy's heart, mind, and experience.

The father never lost hope. He knew that the boy would return. He would not let go. He prayed and waited and hoped. The Heavenly Father can depend on the agencies at work on the prodigal to bring him home. He knows that the Holy Spirit is hovering near to bring him a little nearer every day. The great heart of the Father hopes and yearns and draws the wanderer to Him. Hope never dies in His heart.

The father welcomed the boy with a hearty welcome. That scene is unforgettable: *When he was yet a great way off, his father saw him.* How did he see him at the very moment he came over the hill? His old eyes had been focused on that hillside for a long time. In hope and expectation and yearning he had watched. There the boy was, in sight! *He ran . . . kissed him warmly.* He "smothered him with kisses." Full forgiveness, full welcome, and full restoration to his old place in the heart and in the home was his. The choice robe, the beautiful ring, the best sandals, the fatted calf, the joyous feast—what more could be asked? All this was his because love had its way.

The Heavenly Father saw His beloved prodigal suffer and writhe in agony in the disgraceful surroundings of the far country. He saw him as he made his great decision. He heard him say, "I will arise and go to my father." He understood the depths of his sincere repentance. He heard him as he continued to rehearse his speech of confession. He watched every step of that journey home and listened to the heartfelt confession. The repentance was so genuine and overflowing that it needed no measuring.

Then, in a welcome the like of which human eyes have never witnessed, the Father gathered the soiled sinner to His great arms of love in full forgiveness, in complete cleansing, in plenteous renewal, and in a flood of grace that made the heavens ring with praise and rejoicing. Even the angels, amazed at such a signal display of the "amazing grace," joined in the resounding chorus. It is a great moment in heaven when a wandering child comes home for that glad welcome to the Father's house. Remember that this is the picture Jesus gave us of the Father and His exceeding joy at the conversion of a soul. We cannot begin to know the wonder and glory of it all. We can neither measure nor fathom the love of God. How could those heartless critics stand by and have respect for themselves after this picture? How could they look the Master in the face again?

SIN'S TOLL

Jesus, in painting His picture of the love and compassion and grace of God, has left us a clear appraisal of the work of sin in the life of the boy. Even before he came to his decision to leave the father's house, seeds of disloyalty, discontent, and disrespect had been making inroads into his life. It is a perilous moment when such situations occur. It is especially pathetic when individuals develop such attitudes toward God. These sinful tendencies lead to the experience of the far country.

It was in that country that license and lowered standards and discarded restraints brought him to the brink of ruin. Life there worked havoc in all the realms of the boy's life. The momentum of circumstances took him further. His associates hindered instead of helped. His money made it much easier to go further and further into sin. A spending spree must have carried him far out beyond the line of safety. A youth who had been sheltered and shielded at home was poorly prepared for such currents.

When his possessions were gone he found that he had no friends, no food, no income, no one to counsel. In desperation he turned to one who offered some aid but in reality only pushed him even lower. Days and weeks of servitude, hunger, loneliness, and despair brought him nearer and nearer the place where reason could return and where thoughts of home and the father's house could come to him. He had sinned grievously. He had suffered much. He thought and prayed and made a great resolve. There were not many steps to the lights of home. He resolutely set his face and his feet on the road to the house of his father. He kept on plodding until he arrived at the gate.

THE ELDER SON (25–32)

Then envy reared its ugly head. How thoughtless! How inopportune! Why should envy come to the greatest celebration the old mansion had ever known? The father was happy! The son (the prodigal) was happy. The entire household was rejoicing. Kindliness of heart, sweetness of spirit, warmth of soul, and joyous participation in glad singing were all in evidence. Then a surly, sour, cynical elder brother appeared. He would not come in to the feast. He did not like his father; he had neither love nor respect for his father's other son. Self-righteousness is a terrible sin. The father was greatly troubled by the ugly behavior of his elder son, but could do nothing.

What was wrong with him? Envy and jealousy had grown quickly from an overdose of selfishness. Such unchristianlike fruits have no place in any individual at any time. The elder brother was wrong in every particular because he was wrong in this area of his soul. He was totally out of tune with his father and had been unhappy in his life. His work had been toil and drudgery without any genuine delight. He gave a demonstration of self-centeredness, self-pity, ugly rationalization, and smug complacency in his dealings with others.

He had no gratitude whatever for the blessings that had been his through the gifts and love and kindness of his father. Nothing in his words or his manner gave the slightest indication that he loved his father or had any sympathy for him. He had toiled and struggled, but all for the selfish gratification of his own interests. He refused to show respect or love for his brother. He was not at all pleased that his brother had come home. All his thoughts, words, and attitudes were bad. He is a creature of Jesus' imagination, but there are many people in the world who fit Jesus' description of this older brother perfectly.

As Jesus was speaking, the scribes and Pharisees, who had been ugly in their criticism of Him, must have received this closing paragraph in full force. No one of these words missed its mark. Each was a direct hit. They were the "older brother." They were the ones who hurt the heart of God by their lack of love and concern. Why should they despise the souls of lost men and women about them? Why should they show contempt for repenting sinners? Why should they remonstrate with Jesus for pausing to tell them the way home?

Do you know an "elder brother" anywhere? Are you sure you do not show some slight signs of kinship with him? The Master will know. Let Him look into your heart for evidences.

G. Campbell Morgan quotes Samuel Chadwick as saying from the pulpit, "I am going to preach on the third Son in the parable of the prodigal son." After showing the picture of the younger breaking his father's heart and the elder out of sympathy with his father's heart, he said, "Isn't there another Son? Yes, there is. He is the Man Who was uttering the parable. He was God's Son, His ideal Son on the human level. He never broke God's heart with His sin, but He was so in sympathy with God's heart that He died to save sinners." [2] Jesus is the third Son of the parable of the prodigal.

PUNGENT PREACHING POINTS

The pitiable plight of the sinner as pictured in these parables should make soul-winners of all of us. The lost sheep wanders in perilous wastes instead of enjoying the peace and safety of the green pastures and the still waters. The lost piece of money, its stamp marred, lies buried in dust and darkness. Both are lost beyond hope of recovery.

Powerful encouragement should be given to sinners to accept Christ and find the forgiveness and cleansing and restoration that come when they are received by the Father.

The course of sin is always downward. It begins in a heart destitute of love of God. It turns into selfish seeking for satisfaction. It shows itself as the transgressor who is willing to desecrate all God's holy gifts to sin and shame. Terrible consequences follow—dissatisfaction, unrest, want, misery, remorse, and deeper desecration and degradation.

God often speaks to the sinner through want, famine, and afflictions. The rebellious one may turn to God or turn to more flagrant participation in sin. The picture of the prodigal is truly pathetic. He had spent all, had been sorely disillusioned, had no friends, was hungry, was afflicted by soul famine, and had no hope of a better day. What a desperate plight!

The prodigal's upward steps are important. He came to

---

[2] *The Gospel According to Luke* (New York: Fleming H. Revell Company, 1931), p. 184.

himself; he realized that his sins were against God; he determined to confess and forsake his sins; he got up and made his way home; he opened his heart in full confession; he took full responsibility for all his sin; he felt the arms of his father about him in forgiveness and cleansing.

This parable has awakened us to the tragedy of selfish, self-righteous, sinful behavior on the part of those who claim to be Christians. We should examine ourselves to be sure that we are not like the elder brother. Let us make sure that we do not resemble the critics to whom Jesus preached.

Since the state of the sinner is so pathetic, God is so willing to save, the heavenly hosts are so happy to rejoice over the sinner's salvation, and the joys for the returning prodigals are so precious, our hearts ought to seek to lead them to Christ! May the Holy Spirit direct us to the lost ones and lead us to do our best to show them the way home.

Isaiah LV

Ho, every one that thirsteth, come ye to the waters, and he that hath no money; come ye, buy, and eat; yea, come, buy wine and milk without money and without price. Wherefore do ye spend money for that which is not bread? and your labour for that which satisfieth not? hearken diligently unto me, and eat ye that which is good, and let your soul delight itself in fatness. Incline your ear, and come unto me: hear, and your soul shall live; and I will make an everlasting covenant with you. . . .

Seek ye the Lord while he may be found, call ye upon him while he is near: let the wicked forsake his way, and the unrighteous man his thoughts: and let him return unto the Lord, and he will have mercy upon him; and to our God, for he will abundantly pardon.

VIII. God's Invitation

_____Isaiah LV

HAVE YOU LOST the things money cannot buy? Can you detect any hunger or thirst or any unsatisfied longing? Have you been majoring on minors? What does God see as He looks into your heart? This great chapter, Isaiah 55, will do something for you if you will let it speak its challenge to your heart and mind. Its clear music and its pure gospel will get hold of you. Before you know it you will be under the spell of the poet's penetrating call to repentance and obedience. He represents God as a powerful preacher, going among the people of the market place, urging them to stop and listen and heed the call to spiritual commitment. This passage is an imperious call to get right with God at once.

For a full understanding of the message of this great chapter we need to look back to Isaiah 35 for the picture of the distressing desert, to chapter 40 for the startling announcement of the gospel's being brought into the world, and to chapter 53 for the heart-rending account of the suffering and humiliation endured by the Servant in His work of atonement. Step by step we have been prepared to hear the ringing invitation. All things are now ready. Come to the feast! How happy the prophet is to come with good news and in-

vite every living soul to come to enjoy the bounties prepared!
It is a day of good tidings to weary toilers.

The setting: The words of this chapter were addressed
to Jews who had been living in Babylon for many years. They
had become merchants and traders in exile. Strangely
enough, they liked Babylon. They were successful. They had
settled down to good pagan living. They were feverishly busy
"weighing silver." Each vied with the other in gathering in
shekels and laying by more possessions. In becoming Oriental
traders, they had forgotten that they had been called to be
priests. In their desperate efforts to amass a fortune, they
had lost sight of their call to be God's missionaries to the
people of the world. Instead of devoted witnesses for Jehovah, they had become worldly traders seeking to get rather
than to give. The picture was pathetic. How it must have
hurt the heart of God! His chosen representatives were
worldly "getters." He could see into their barren hearts and
detect the hungers, the thirsts, the needs. He determined to
preach to them and awaken the hungers that could lead to
higher living. He knew that these new-found things did not
satisfy and that deep in the heart were thirsts that He
alone could satisfy. The return of His people would be worth
the effort.

God was seeking to bless the world through them. They
would be worthless as missionaries until they came back to
feed on spiritual food. Cyrus was about to make his move.
Babylon would be taken. The captives would be released to
go back to Zion. God wanted worthy representatives as they
made their way to the old city of Jerusalem. Only as they
put first things first and gave primacy to the spiritual could
He hope to have true messengers.

The outline: The chapter is so beautiful, so exquisite, so
complete, that one hesitates to try to break it up into sepa-

rate bits. One great expositor calls attention to verses one and two as giving the conditions of the desert or the wilderness, and verses ten through thirteen as describing the conditions in God's wonderful garden. Verses three through nine tell of God's appointed way out of the wilderness and into God's garden. This commentator emphasizes the contrast between the first picture and the last.

We might also think of verses one through five as being a divine invitation to all the rich blessings to be found at God's bountiful table, and verses six through thirteen as an announcement of the wonders of God's salvation that is ready. Another way to examine the chapter would be to study it verse by verse through the invitation, the remonstrance, the divine directions, the Messiah, the missionary ideal, the specific demands, the glowing promises, the colorful illustrations, and the power and effectiveness of God's Word.

The invitation: Jehovah invited these worldly men and women to check up and see that they were losing the things that money could not buy. They were making plenty of money. They were buying freely the things they imagined could satisfy. They were going feverishly along, driving themselves to meet fierce competition in order that more things might be bought.

Look at some of the words He used to describe their hearts' needs: *Thirsteth . . . ye spend money for that which is not bread, your labour for that which satisfieth not.* He is picturing hunger, thirst, disappointment, disillusionment, and soul decay. The people had money and were spending it freely, but they had no money that could buy soul food, soul satisfaction. All their "things" still left them thirsty, hungry, and unsatisfied. Our Lord touches on this when he describes the rich man with his new barns who said to his soul, "Thou hast much goods laid up for many years; take thine ease, eat, drink, and be merry" (Luke 12:19). Imagine the soul being able to eat corn and beans and wheat and barley! That man had the wrong idea about food for a soul. Corn could never satisfy.

The preacher in verse one is declaring that the gospel is God's answer for all the inner cravings of man's heart. That heart was divinely created with thirsts, yearnings, and hungers that can find satisfaction only in Him and in gifts from His lavish hand. This verse is a universal call to thirsty ones of all lands, all times, all ages. The dust of material things can choke, and the lack of satisfying water makes living impossible. The true way to life and soul-satisfaction lies in heeding the call to "come to the waters." One who has sold his soul for gold needs to let the eternal Evangelist take his hand and lead him to the bubbling springs of the water of life. The wells of salvation are open, adequate, satisfying, eternally effective, and gloriously refreshing.

Do you say with the psalmist, "My soul thirsts for God, for the living God" (Psalm 42:2) ? Are you conscious of that thirst? If the food that you have been eating and the water that you have been drinking have left you without refreshment and without nourishment, you can well stop in your tracks and listen to the clear animated voice of the announcer: *Ho, everyone that thirsteth!* His call is a direct call to you. It is God's way of making clear to you something of a real thirst that needs exactly what our Lord can supply.

The water: (Cf. Isaiah 12:3 and 41:18). The thirsty, penniless, desperate ones are called to the reservoir of life-giving water. The prophet reminds them that broken cisterns will fail them in the moment of dire need. They cannot still gnawing hunger or the burning thirst of the soul. All the people and their needs are included. The invitation extends to the last person on earth. It reaches any thirsty or needy soul—to the remotest bounds of God's creation.

Water, wine, milk are all offered. Water revives and refreshes; wine lightens and gladdens; milk nourishes and gives strength. These three things cover all the needs of the body as a man of Palestine would know them. Surely our Lord makes it clear that every possible need of the soul is found plentifully in Him. "He that cometh to me shall never hunger; and he that believeth on me shall never thirst" (John 6:35). He knows the needs and the remedy. He offers it freely.

The protest: Bluntly and powerfully the preacher speaks of the utter folly of lavishing effort and toil and money on poor, useless, tasteless bread that fails to satisfy. These people were putting forth endless effort in a vain attempt to buy soul satisfaction. They were unmindful of the silly spectacle they were making. The divine voice called them back to think soberly and check on themselves. They were missing the things that money could not buy.

It has always been difficult to impress men with the fact that the things money cannot purchase are the real food, drink, and satisfaction of the inner man. This evangelist sought in faraway Babylon to have men pause in their mad rush long enough to see that thirsty souls could easily starve without the specially prepared food designed for soul growth. When will we get this eternally fresh concept clearly in our minds? When will we realize that life without God is the poorest bit of existence with thirst, hunger, restlessness, want, and unsatisfied longings as constant companions? Feverishness and confusion join with true starvation to reveal a lack of the peace, poise, and power that every soul should be able to claim as God's gift.

Paul, in the book of Romans, reveals some of the rich

treasures that come rolling into the life of a man that comes to the Saviour for the water of life. He lists justification, peace with God, absence of fear, freedom from the power of sin, a vital sense that God is Father, a reduced estimate of suffering, a transformed prayer life, assurance of ultimate and certain victory, and the presence and power of the Holy Spirit.

The word "spend" is literally "weigh silver." A literal rendering of "your labor" would be "your earnings." These people in Babylon were putting forth unusual efforts and driving themselves to find that which could satisfy. (Cf. Jer. 2:13).

Assurance: How plantively the Lord called to them to listen, to think on their way, to obey the divine call! He hastened to assure them that their poor starved souls should be feasting on food that would produce the greatest delight. Those souls had been undernourished so long that they had deteriorated and had lost the blessed enjoyment that should have been theirs. He has spiritual food ready for anyone who will come and eat.

How sorely needed this call is for our generation! How many lean, starving souls are about us! His plenteous grace is available. How thrilling the call to come for the unpurchasable treasures designed for the fullest enjoyment! Money is able to buy so many delightful things that we are tempted to forget the eternally satisfying food for the soul which will always be among the things money can never buy. In the quiet of your secret place, will you take an inventory and see if you are the person the preacher is addressing in this paragraph? You may be sure that God's mercy and His love and His abounding grace are all ready for your acceptance.

The everlasting covenant promised: The prophet begged the people to stretch out their ears in attention, get on their feet and start walking, hear with interest and obedience, and begin real living again. The condition imposed was simply the full submission of the will to the divine will. It sounds exceedingly simple and easy. Note the verbs "listen," "come," "hear," "live." Salvation has always been so conditioned. The Old Testament and the New are together in putting this divine treasure within the reach of every person. The plan is simple; yet it is definite enough to be plainly a step-by-step process. Salvation is always a clear act of the will, never a bargaining matter. It is simple acceptance of the priceless gift God has proffered. The terms are set down by God Himself, and the human being must move into the position decreed for him. The soul needs to have a miracle performed by the divine hand so it can begin living again. (Cf. Paul's words in Ephesians 2:1-5, 11-13). It is tragic to find souls that were created to *live,* going on with a disease fatal to the soul. Jesus said, "I am come that they might have life, and that they might have it more abundantly" (John 10:10). He is ever seeking to make the soul live so that life may be abundant.

For generations God had promised the eternal covenant. Here that promise was again renewed. Jeremiah had some majestic things to say about this everlasting covenant (31: 31-34). The New Testament gives the conclusion on the matter.

A witness: The Messiah was one definitely appointed by the divine Father. He was to do the work of a witness of Jehovah's faithfulness and power and to be Ruler or Prince among the people of the earth. Through travail He is to come to triumph. Isaiah makes it clear that God is working out His plans for world redemption through a Person, the Suffering Servant, who will become the powerful commander of the people. Their attention is arrested and set on the Person who makes atonement possible and who takes over the full leadership of the redeemed ones of the earth. As a result of His divine ministry, His death on the cross, and His leadership, the sons of Israel who come to the Saviour will be able to take up again their mission of bringing the good news to other nations.

The urgent call: The words "seek" and "call" are beautiful. The preacher has urged the people to listen and look. Now he would have them put forth activity and go in search of God. There is no intimation that He will be hard to find. He is quite near. Calling out to Him is an essential act showing a man's interest, his concern, and his willingness to let blessings come into his life. The essential parts of repentance are involved in these words.

The words "while He may be found" and "while He is near" certainly imply that there are times when it is much easier to find salvation. There will come times when God will have moved away and left the rebellious one in his lost condition. One sins away his day of grace. In Hosea we have the words, "Ephraim is joined to idols: let him alone" (Hos. 4:17). To be sure, God loves and wants to save, but rejected and spurned love finally comes to the breaking point. The beautiful thing in our text is the assurance that He is near and that He can be found. What a glorious assurance! (Cf. Jer. 29:12–13; Isa. 49:8.)

How may one seek the Lord? The voice declares that the man of evil or falsehood must *forsake his way* and *turn unto the Lord.* Human responsibility involves a complete turning away from the present way of thinking and doing. Both realms must be completely reversed. The mind, the purpose, and the conduct of a saved man must be completely changed. Faces that were turned earthward must be turned heavenward. Repentance, faith, and obedience must all be in evidence. The Greek word *metanoia* might be used here as the germ of the New Testament doctrines of repentance are enunciated. We see what man must do to qualify for the gifts from God's hand.

God's promises: We are assured that God has a part to play in the transaction when man has shown his willingness to repent and be obedient. Assuming that man has done all that he can do, the divine activity makes victory certain. *He will have mercy. . . . He will abundantly pardon.* The eternal God who is "plenteous in mercy" will reveal the love He has for man. That revelation will be expressed in multiplied pardons. The forgiveness from God will be so abundant and so complete that the pardons will be heaped up on each other in lavish fashion.

True love has a way of expressing itself without stint. The father of the prodigal son (Luke 15) certainly did not strain out a mere token gift to the boy. He gave recklessly and freely. Love dictated the giving. Men in Old Testament days were assured of such treatment at the hands of a loving Father who looked longingly for the penitent return of His beloved creatures. How beautifully the gospel was preached in the market places of Babylon, in the streets of Jerusalem! How wondrous are His words of invitation to people of Houston, Los Angeles, Louisville, New York, Montreal, London, or Tokyo today. The faintest call of a troubled child is heard instantly and clearly by the Father who cares and seeks and waits. His rich promise is as sweet and precious and true today as at any time in all history.

The exalted One: If a man is unwilling to give up his ways and his thoughts, he needs to be made conscious of the presence of the exalted One. God's thoughts and His ways are too vast and too sublime to be measured by the earth-bound conceptions of men. These verses furnish a good compelling reason for repentance as well as a reason for an expectant hope.

Contrast the scenes described in these last verses with the fitful, feverish scenes of the earlier verses where men and women strove excitedly in a wild scramble to get money and to spend it. That view of sordidness, barrenness, and strife in the world markets left us sick at heart. In these stately lines we are led into God's beautiful outdoors where stars, star cities, and boundless areas of transcendent beauty lift us into heights that are indescribable.

God's thoughts, His purposes of redemption, and His ways are so high and exalted that mere finite men have difficulty grasping their full meaning. Even though infinitely sublime, His thoughts and ways can be understood and appreciated by one who has come in genuine repentance to learn of Him and to be filled with His knowledge. God is near and wants to reveal Himself fully and completely. He has set in motion the many ways of giving to human beings the richer revelation so that penitent ones might come to know Him and His thoughts and His ways.

The reason there is so much difference between God's thoughts and men's thoughts is that men are not right with God. They are incurably at variance with God. The direction of their thoughts, characters, and lives is out of line with God. When a careful study of God's blueprint for life is made along with the actual trend and growth of life, the result is heart-rending. When the sinner sees the true state of his heart and falls on his face in sincere repentance, he is immediately ready for pardon, redemption, and renewal. He passes from the desert into the garden. He is now able to think God's thoughts after Him and fit into His plans for life.

Rain, snow, Word: How might the people know that rich

gifts would be bestowed? Isaiah pictures beautifully the ministry of rain and snow and fertile soil in bringing a harvest to delight the hearts of men. Immediately we are reminded that God's Word acts in the same manner. Rain and snow and earth produce harvests. God's revelation plus human obedience produce life's most beautiful fruitfulness. Thus God brings about His highest will and produces trophies of grace.

Moses said, "Man shall not live by bread alone, but by every word that proceedeth out of the mouth of God" (Deut. 8:3). One cannot easily live in the desert when existing on bread alone. For life's richest fulness one must add the ingredient described as the Word of God. Just as the rain and snow refuse to turn back to the clouds until God's purpose has been accomplished, even so the Word of God cannot fail in its mission of mercy. It will bring about the victory. When it comes into barren souls and lives, it turns barrenness into rich harvest. It quickens powers of fruitfulness. It supplies nourishment to needy souls. It provides guidance at the forks of the road. It comforts troubled hearts. It heartens those who lack courage and confidence. Gently and silently it turns barren souls into fruitful ones.

Joy: When this transformation has come about by the power of the Word of God in men's hearts, the people will be ready for its fruits in human lives. The promise declares that the new man will go out and be led forth with joy and with peace. Joy fills the heart. Anxiety and fear are gone.

A holy peace fills the mind and heart. Jehovah is the leader. All nature joins in the thunderous applause. Perhaps for the soul thoroughly immersed in the dust such rejoicing may seem out of place, but it is God's way of bringing home to the heart of those who are in tune with nature the boundless resources and the heart-filling joys of the ones led by His hand. Thanks be to God for the grand assurances of the eternal delights flowing from His touch into hearts and minds that have become His through the atoning death of His Son.

Conclusion: Look again at the pathetic picture of busy, jumpy, striving men buying and selling and joining in fierce competition in order to amass the things that will purchase other desirable things. Listen to Jesus as He says, "Lay not up for yourselves treasures upon earth, where moth and rust doth corrupt, and where thieves break through and steal: but lay up for yourselves treasures in heaven, where neither moth nor rust doth corrupt, and where thieves do not break through nor steal: for where your treasure is, there will your heart be also" (Matt. 6:19–20).

Think for a moment of the urgent, insistent call of God to sinning men. None are too vile. None have gone too far away. The living Father makes His invitation open and inviting to everyone. Listen to Jesus: "Come unto me, all ye that labour and are heavy laden, and I will give you rest" (Matt. 11:28). "Him that cometh to me I will in no wise cast out" (John 6:37).

Listen to the word concerning soul-living: "And thy soul shall live" (Jer. 38:20). How beautiful it is! Our eternal Father is never happy over sick souls or diseased souls. He ever calls us to come to Him for that which makes the soul abundantly alive.

Repentance and salvation have two sides: *Seek . . . call . . . forsake . . . return . . . have mercy . . . multiply . . . pardon.* The Holy Spirit helps man with his part. In love and mercy God comes with His part.

G. Campbell Morgan says: "Verse seven may be described as the wicket gate through which men pass from the desert to the garden. It is so marvelously and simply hung that the weakest and most paralyzed hand touching it, swings it toward the garden, but that wicket gate is hinged on Calvary's cross."

The great call to repentance (verses 6–7) forms a clear-cut dividing range. In the verses preceding this call we see men bending beneath the load of heartaches and hardships, seeking breathlessly to muddle through and find some measure of pleasure and satisfaction. They are plodding on, with God left out of their lives. How pathetic! Following these verses we are in a new world altogether. Freedom, joy, peace, hope, satisfaction, and gladsome praise have brought light and laughter and love to bless hearts and to make effective their witness. They have found their life in God. With the happy Christian of New Testament days they can say, "Whereas I was blind, now I see" (John 9:25).

How can one go on in sin and selfishness when such incredible wonders await each one who turns to God, who trusts fully in the Lord Jesus Christ as Saviour? Joys unspeakable are his as he lays his trembling hand in the nail-pierced hand. Hallelujah, what a Saviour!

> I heard the voice of Jesus say,
> "Come unto Me and rest;
> Lay down, thou weary one, lay down
> Thy head upon My breast."
>
> I came to Jesus as I was,
> Weary, and worn, and sad;
> I found in Him a restingplace,
> And He has made me glad.
>
> HORATIUS BONAR

Romans VIII

There is therefore now no condemnation to them which are in Christ Jesus, who walk not after the flesh, but after the Spirit. . . . Now if any man have not the Spirit of Christ, he is none of his. . . . If the Spirit of him that raised up Jesus from the dead dwell in you, he that raised up Christ from the dead shall also quicken your mortal bodies by his Spirit that dwelleth in you. . . . The Spirit himself beareth witness with our spirit, that we are the children of God: and if children, then heirs; heirs of God, and joint-heirs with Christ. . . . The Spirit also helpeth our infirmities: for we know not what we should pray for as we ought: but the Spirit himself maketh intercession for us. . . . And we know that all things work together for good to them that love God, to them who are the called according to his purpose. . . .

He that spared not his own Son, but delivered him up for us all, how shall he not with him also give us all things? . . .

Nay, in all these things we are more than conquerors through him that loved us. For I am persuaded, that neither death, nor life, nor angels, nor principalities, nor powers, nor things present, nor things to come, nor height, nor depth, nor any other creature, shall be able to separate us from the love of God, which is in Christ Jesus our Lord.

IX. More Than Conquerors

DO YOU KNOW the riches of Paul's letter to the Romans? Have you studied it to learn what Christianity's greatest interpreter of the deep things of Christ has to say about the gospel and its power? Has the full force of Christ's mighty work in redemption gripped your soul? Are you acquainted with the place and power of the Holy Spirit? Do you know Him? Does He live and work in you? What does He do? What are you doing about sin in your life? These and many other pertinent questions come to us when we open this significant portion of New Testament writing.

The letter to the Romans is clearly written. You can read it and see into the meaning of each line. You will learn much that is new and startling. The doctrinal sections will intrigue you. The practical sections will amaze you. The long-range pictures of the other shore will moisten your eyes. Hope, certainty, assurance, faith, peace of mind, power in prayer, and victorious living will be yours. The Holy Spirit wants to live victoriously in you.

Paul knew the Lord Jesus Christ as his own personal Saviour. He knew what it meant to be _in Christ_. He wanted all men to know of the peace that comes to one who is in Christ.

He interpreted the meaning of that theme with clarity and persuasiveness. He made it clear that eternal peace was the gift of Christ to all sinful men who would submit their lives to Him.

In Romans 7 Paul revealed something of the terrific struggle that goes on in the mind of one who has allied himself with Christ but still finds that both he and the Holy Spirit must live in the old body that is definitely lined up with the devil. Sin holds a powerful grip on the flesh. Sin is an active power at war with the Holy Spirit. What actually happens is that the presence of the Holy Spirit stirs up a real conflict with sin in the body. Paul declared that there was always spiritual tension in his heart. He sided with the Holy Spirit and hated sin. In the agony of his continual struggle he cried out, "O wretched man that I am! Who will rescue me out of the body of this death?" (7:24). In a moment he caught his breath and answered his own question: "Thanks be to God through Jesus Christ our Lord." In these great verses Paul has been giving the personal illustration of his journey through justification and sanctification toward glorification. He wants it fully understood that we are all utterly helpless in obtaining victory over sin in our own strength and by our own efforts. He is certain that victory is possible through the power of the Holy Spirit.

VICTORIOUS LIVING (1–17)

The atmosphere in chapter eight is different. The struggle has given way to quiet trust. Peace reigns. Yes, there is struggle, but the Holy Spirit has been given so much wholehearted support that sin has been beaten back. Paul believes in sanctification. He is not willing to let that lovely old word and the words "holy" and "holiness" be shelved for the private use of men and women who claim them as their own special property. The apostle assures us that for the one who is *in Christ,* sanctification or holy living is possible and necessary. It is a privilege, but it is also an obligation. You may—more, you must—live a holy life. The Holy Spirit in the heart and life makes all the difference. Victorious living could never be accomplished except through His power. With His presence and power, the one in Christ may demonstrate a life of victory and holiness. It is the Spirit's victory, but He enables you and me to be the victors.

No condemnation . . . no separation (1, 39): We are literally thrilled in heart to see the first and last words of this great chapter framing the wondrous treasures of God's revelation to needy hearts. We might look through these verses and find something of this order: "No condemnation . . . no slavery . . . no sin (left in the heart) . . . no more enmity against God . . . no more death . . . no fear . . . no more orphans . . . no more poverty . . . no failure in prayer . . . no loss . . . no separation." It is a shout of victory. Christ has, through His atoning death, redeemed us from our guilt and the power of sin. The debt has all been canceled. The ransom price has been paid. We are in Christ Jesus. This news is truly good news. No message by telephone or telegraph could bring a more welcome pronouncement than that verse.

God, sending his own Son . . . condemned sin (3): Paul's clear statement that sin no longer rests upon men was based on the great theological fact that God has done something about it. Sin and death and the devil held sway in the world. Men were helpless and hopeless as sin had dominion over them. No human power could break away the chains of slavery forged by the devil. No rebellion against his power could be successful. No determination to live a righteous life could do anything to change the situation. Every man was guilty and condemned before a holy God. Condemnation loomed high and forbidding as the sinner saw it confronting him. What could be done? Who would come to the rescue of enslaved men and women?

God came in the person of the Son, Jesus Christ, to take upon Himself sinful flesh and, because of a sinless life, He was able to present Himself as the Lamb of God. At Calvary He made the supreme sacrifice and wrote the condemnation on sin, once for all. He became our sin-offering. His sacrifice was propitiatory and vicarious; it was for us. God the Father sent; Christ the Son came and suffered and died, setting us free from the law of sin. How happy we ought to be! What a momentous deed it was! Nothing will ever equal it until He comes again. His redemption is a plenteous redemption.

To them that are in Christ Jesus (1): What a wealth of rich treasures is heaped up in the treasure room of the one who is in Christ! Justification by faith is the beginning. The old account is fully settled. There is *no condemnation*. The shackles, forged by the devil, have been broken off. The peace that passes all understanding is the divine gift to the believer. He is "sealed," is accepted, has the forgiveness of sins, has redemption through His blood, has an inheritance, is His workmanship, is an heir of God, and is eternally kept by the power of God. Again and again we shall shout our praises heavenward, that we are new creatures in Christ.

Walk . . . after the Spirit (4): Here we have the secret of that sinless life, that sanctification, that victory. Paul is making it clear to us in verses 1–11 that such a life of victory is possible. The Holy Spirit comes into our lives first to convict, then to bring us to Christ, then to bring about regeneration. He then takes up His life in us to enable us to be free from sin's dominion. With the Holy Spirit in us we can walk and obey and live a holy life. "Sin shall not have dominion over you" (6:14).

Paul tells us that Christ died, not merely to bring forgiveness to us and to save us from hell and from the consequences of our sins, but *that the righteousness of the law might be fulfilled in us* (4). To Titus he said, "That he might separate unto himself a peculiar people, zealous of good works" (2:14). Christ wants us to be positively righteous and to stand righteous beings before God.

The Holy Spirit is called "the Spirit of life" because He is the giver of love, peace, joy, and the bountiful life promised by our Saviour. He is the great giver of sanctification. He sees to it that the Christian grows and struggles and measures up to the Father's purpose and ideal for him.

If any man have not the Spirit of Christ, he is none of his (9) : What does Paul mean by that striking statement? Does it strike home to your heart? Do you honestly think you can qualify? Let us remember that if we are not in Christ, we are dead in sin and no human agent can bring us back to life. If we are not in Christ, all is lost—unless we do something at once. If we are Christians only when we have the Spirit of Christ, then it is exceedingly important that we have Him. He must live in us. We must be indwelt by the Holy Spirit. He comes in when we become Christians through personal faith in Jesus Christ.

How then may we know beyond the slightest question of doubt that we have the Holy Spirit in our hearts? Paul tells us in verse five that when He is present the individual *minds the things of the Spirit*. In verse 7 he declares that the Christian is *not at enmity against God.* In verse 14 he says that the believer is *led by the Holy Spirit.* In verse 16 he says, *The Spirit himself beareth witness with our spirit that we are the children of God.* You may ask: "What is my attitude toward God?" "What is my conduct?" "How do I live?" Remember those solemn words: *If any man have not the Spirit of Christ, he is none of his.* If He is in your heart, it will be an easy matter to be sure of His presence. If He is not in your heart, you can settle the matter at once. Trust Him fully and confess Him as Saviour and Lord. "Let go and let God have His wonderful way."

The Spirit . . . quicken your mortal bodies (11): Paul has revealed the sad fact concerning the body that it has also been brought under the "law of sin and death." Physical death is one of the consequences of sin which God has permitted to remain for the Christian. In verse 10 the apostle tells us that although our bodies were death-stricken by the fall, our spirits are gloriously alive in Christ. He further assures us that this righteousness engendered by the Holy Spirit (within us) gives the pledge of a glorious resurrection for the body. *He that raised up Christ from the dead shall also quicken your mortal bodies by his Spirit that dwelleth in you* (11). Christ was *raised up.* Human bodies must be quickened or made alive. Life must be communicated before the body is raised up. Note Paul's use of this idea in another epistle: "As in Adam all die, even so in Christ shall all be made alive" (1 Cor. 15:22). We know that both the spirit and the mortal body of the believer are safe *by his Spirit that dwelleth in you.*

So then . . . we are debtors (12): In verses 1–11 Paul has unveiled for us our privileges in Christ. We can live the holy life. Sanctification is possible. In these verses (12–17) we are confronted with the obligation to be holy and to move to complete sanctification. Holiness is a duty, a debt. We are rich in the treasures that abide. They are ours because of the death of Christ and through the indwelling presence of the Holy Spirit. We are free from the law of sin and death, but we are "in debt" to Him who has freed us. Our obligation is to walk with Him in victorious living. Nothing short of that high standard will please Him. We are eternally indebted to walk as the Spirit leads.

So often we have considered holiness a high, almost inaccessible peak, too difficult for any except a few choice spirits to reach. Paul brings holiness down to daily living and declares that this is His will, even the sanctification of every one of us. Paul makes it clear that striving for holiness is a sacred, binding duty for all those who name the name of Christ. The ideal is attainable because we have the Holy Spirit continually within.

Ye shall live (13): Is this what our Lord meant when he said, "I am come that they might have life, and that they might have it more abundantly" (John 10:10)? Our eternal Saviour bought salvation at such a cost and loved His precious people so devotedly that He wanted them to have and enjoy life in its richest proportions. Paul describes the new life under the guidance of the Holy Spirit as being full living. *Ye shall live!* Temptations, burdens, sufferings, struggles, exacting climbs, battles, and every other experience will be but constituent elements in the exhibition of victorious living made possible by His encouragement. He has provided abundant living for you. The Holy Spirit guarantees the full life for every Christian who will let Him bring it to pass.

Led by the Spirit of God . . . sons of God (14): What a lift it gives us to know that life is not drudgery nor slavery nor toilsome plodding but exhilarating adventure under the personal guidance of the third Person of the Godhead. The Spirit gladly accepts our willingness to follow and leads us in the way that makes for victory. It is only as we yield ourselves to His leadership that we can be called God's sons. The human mind cannot comprehend all the glories inherent in that blessed relationship. We are *in Christ.* The Holy Spirit lives and moves in us. We are the sons of God.

Adoption . . . abba, Father . . . children of God (15–16): How beautiful are the unfolding treasures in Christ Jesus! The trustful intimacy reserved for those who are led by the Spirit brings joys indescribable. *Adoption* follows; the Christian is officially and eternally a member of God's family. Imagine the sweetness of being accepted as a *teknia* or "born child" of God. These words combine to picture the delights, the beauties, and the precious intimacy of that relationship in Christ. The Holy Spirit comes with all His authority to bear witness with our human spirits that we are actually "born children" of God. There is kinship, resemblance, character likeness, and similarity of thought and purpose and hope revealed in that figure. We become His children through the new birth.

Heirs . . . joint-heirs (17): The vital sense that the believer has of God as his own Heavenly Father causes him to gasp with breathless wonder as he realizes that the divine inheritance is his and that, along with the Lord Jesus, he is to share in the treasures of heaven. Because of the gospel Paul was a new person. He was no more like the selfish, ambitious, grasping, natural man of those early days than day is like the night. He was a new man in Christ. As a result of his new relationship, we find in his life love, joy, peace, patience, kindness, goodness, faithfulness, gentleness, self-control. These qualities are those of one who has anchored himself in a new relationship. He is a *child* of God, an *heir* of God. The Holy Spirit lives in and rules him. He is literally another person, for he has been born into the family of God. The qualities of his new Father in heaven are the qualities that are prominent in his thoughts, his words, his deeds, and his attitudes. If we share Christ's sufferings, we may be certain that we will share His glory and His treasures.

What more could make a Christian ready to major on living the holy life? Paul has made us want to measure up fully. We are eager to take the obligation to walk with the Spirit and lead a holy life. We long to find full holiness of life as He leads.

PATIENCE UNDER SUFFERING (18–30)

Paul wants us to share in the glory enjoyed by our Saviour. He always seeks to remind us of the good things that await us "down the road." The heavenly glory of the Christ is unbelievably wonderful. No one can imagine the extent or beauty of it. In preparation for full enjoyment of His glory, Paul urges us to be patient in the sufferings that will be ours.

These sufferings will be big and hard and painful and forbidding, but the whole total of them all, rolled into one mighty bundle, will be nothing as compared with the glory which is to be revealed. Everything all the Christians of all the ages endure for Christ's sake will be but a very small thing compared to the heavenly glory to be shared by all who are *heirs of God*. What a glory it must be!

Paul pictures all nature, painfully aware of grievous limitations since the sin in the garden, as breaking forth with inexpressible longings for that hour of divine manifestation when she shall share that which corresponds to the great resurrection. In that blessed day God's creation shall be released from its burden of decay, disappointment, and corruption to share with redeemed men the emancipation which constitutes the future glory of the children of God. The whole cosmos is involved in man's redemption, and all of creation will share in the glory that is to come to Christ.

The groans and yearnings of Christians point in the same direction and predict satisfaction too precious for words as the full glory of Christ is revealed. Fulfilled will be the hopes, longings, and prayers of the sons of God through the centuries. The apostle is strangely aware that the fullest enjoyment of God's richest promises cannot come until spirit and body are both delivered from the dark traces of the "fall," until Christ has had heaped upon Him the glory that has been eternally in the heart of the Father.

Daringly the writer calls for *patience* in the upward struggle. Patience is a masterful quality—terrifically strong, high, and Christlike. Every step will call out loudly for it. Every burden will need its presence. Every moment of persecution, every agony, every pain, every hard struggle, and every passing year will beg for patience. Paul's plea for it is pathetic, but noble and beautiful. We look hopefully to the hour of the complete realization of our *adoption:* the full redemption of the church and the public bestowal upon our Lord of the glory that was His from the foundation of the world. We wait patiently!

The Spirit helpeth (26): In addition to his argument that future glory is to be great, Paul urges patience because of the exceptional helpfulness of the Holy Spirit. *He helpeth!* In our weakness and helplessness we find the unfailing hand of our Helper constantly giving aid. The picture is that of one reaching in from the other side carrying His part of every load. He actually helps.

We know not how to pray (26): It is in the realm of effective praying that we are weakest. Paul assures us that the Holy Spirit makes up for all the lack. His intercessions are included along with ours and help interpret to the Father the deeper yearnings of our hearts. *He that searches the heart knows what is in the mind of the Spirit.* We have the divine Intercessor who teaches us how to pray and helps us to present our petitions *according to the will of God.*

All things work together for good (28): God is in full and complete control. Verses twenty-nine and thirty should precede verse twenty-eight in our interpretation. We are to be *conformed to the image of his Son.* God has a plan, a purpose. He has complete specifications written for His *children,* those who *love God* and are *called according to his purpose.* He is in constant touch with them. He keeps, guides, sustains, comforts, and empowers His own through the constant ministry of the Holy Spirit. How could anything be more true than Paul's simple appraisal of God's working?

Again we come back to the life under the leading of the Spirit. The Spirit's working makes all the difference. God's eternal purpose must prevail. That purpose is actively worked out in inducing the child of God to love Him and to let his life be lived according to the will of God. Children of God can know beyond question that a personal God wants everything to work in the harmonious way Paul describes. How comforting to have a Father who has absolute power, eternal purpose, and a personal love for us! It is His will that we shall fit perfectly into His plan for His world.

His called ones (29–30): Paul makes it clear that there are conditions to be met. Let us follow him through these two glorious verses and gain an insight into the divine purpose in bringing men from justification through sanctification to full glorification. May we reach back into eternity to see the mind, will, and purpose of God at work on His plans for His people and His world.

Foreknew. Paul has in mind the divine decision as to what He would do for individuals in the working out of His purpose. He looked upon them with favor as He visualized their possibilities and potentialities as living "stones" in His building.

Foreordained. God set these chosen ones apart beforehand as individuals to be conformed to the image of His Son. Imagine the dignity and honor of such a selection! Are you aware of the eternal significance of God's choice of you? God thought you would be able to become His ideal man and fit into His redemptive purpose (Eph. 1:4–12).

Called. The purpose of God for the individual formed in eternity is held on through the ages. Finally the hour comes when the individual has the "tap on his shoulder" and is persuasively led by the Holy Spirit to the One who has redeemed him (cf. John 6:44; 15:16).

Justified. When individuals respond to His call, they become *new creatures in Christ*. G. Campbell Morgan describes this action: "Justification is the re-instatement of the soul of man in such relationship and actual fellowship with God, as that soul would have occupied had there never been any sin, had there never been any guilt." [1]

Glorified. The same great author says, "Man resuming finally his true place in the universe of God, lifts again, to the place it has fallen, groaning, sighing, sobbing creation." [2] The saved man comes into the fullest realization of God's purposes and plans for him and shares eternal glory with his Saviour, the Lord Jesus. He is truly conformed to the image of the Son (cf. Phil. 3:12, 21; 1 Cor. 15:49).

Thus we have looked for a fleeting moment on the eternal

---

[1] *Living Messages of the Books of the Bible* (New York: Fleming H. Revell Co., 1912) , p. 104.
[2] *Ibid.*

purpose of Almighty God. The sight is almost too much for us, and yet it is challenging. We realize that we have been chosen by our Father to come by way of justification to full glorification as we are led and kept by the Holy Spirit. Are you on your way to fulfilling the purpose of God for your life?

GOLDEN ASSURANCE (31–39)

All the way along we have had divinely given notes of assurance. It has been extremely heartening to climb with the inspired apostle through so many changing scenes and to experience breath-taking views as new areas of truth open before us. The Holy Spirit led Paul into high and challenging revelations of God's love, purpose, and glorious promises. At this point in the chapter we are brought up suddenly with some pointed questions which call us to express ourselves in the light of these rich truths.

Who can stand against us? Of course, it is clear that there is no power anywhere that can match strength with the eternal God. He is supreme. He is all powerful. No power can stand against Him. No power will dare try.

Does He love us? This question calls out the greatest verse found in all Paul's writings: "He that spared not His own Son, but delivered him up for us all, how shall he not with him also freely give us all things?" (8:32). Such love as that stands as the best proof imaginable of the fathomless love of God for us. Such love will always seek new ways to bless and enrich those who are the objects of that love. Abraham gave a good example in refusing to hold back his only son, Isaac. God, the Father, gave His only Son to die an awful expiatory death to bring redemption to the sons of men. The Father's love surpasses all bounds of thought and understanding.

Who shall separate us from the love of Christ? Immediately Paul's mind runs to the cruel foes of the Christian. Can the believer be sure of the holding power of the Christ? Is the Christian safe in Christ's hand? The foes are tribulation, perplexity, persecution, famine, nakedness, peril, and the sword. Any one of these might be destructive and cruel; any one might be thought powerful enough to cause frail Christians to be sundered from Christ. Paul shouts the denial in these great words: *Nay, in all these things we are more than conquerors through him that loved us.* It is difficult to imagine a more triumphant sentence. Paul used the word *"nikomen,"* meaning "we conquer," that could have been used by Alexander or Xerxes or Cyrus. With it he joined the little word *huper* and created a word to express the feeling of victory that he had at that moment. He wrote, "We are super-conquerors," or *more than conquerors*. What a true statement of the status of one who is in Christ and who has the constant presence of the Holy Spirit.

We claim that heartening sentence today as we bear life's heavy burdens, as we meet the cunning tempter, as we seek to deal with paralyzing fear, as we find ourselves racked with pain, as we need power for witnessing, and as we approach the end of the earthly journey. In each of these situations, life can witness "super-conquerors" as the Holy Spirit empowers for victory. We can shout for joy as we encounter these and many other difficult struggles. Paul assures us that nothing can avail to break us or defeat us or tear us away from the Master's grip on our lives. And we remember that Jesus said, "I give unto them eternal life; and they shall never perish, neither shall any man pluck them out of my hand. . . . No man is able to pluck them out of my Father's hand" (John 10:28–29) .

Are you a conqueror? Is there any likelihood that something will pull you down and write "defeat" across your forehead? What is your estimate of His power in guaranteeing victory instead of defeat? In all of life let us remember that Jesus said, "Lo, I am with you alway" (Matt. 28:20). Does it help to know that you are not alone? Are you made strong by the assurance that He is present at every moment, day and night? Jesus wants you to be victorious. Paul says you can. The presence of the Holy Spirit makes victory a foregone conclusion. *Hupernikomen!*

For I am persuaded (38): This verse is the "great persuasion." Paul, the powerful theologian with the logical mind and the keen understanding of the value of evidence, breaks forth in a tremendous shout of rejoicing. He is convinced. He is certain that the love of Christ is an eternal surety for the soul that is in Christ. No wedge can be driven between them. Every conceivable enemy and power has been introduced and dismissed as wholly inadequate. The Christian is safe and secure, eternally, in Christ.

Neither death nor life: These two formidable foes, representing all the experiences of time and eternity, cannot bring to bear any influence that will break the believer's union with the love of Christ. These things can separate us from friends, loved ones, and possessions, but they can only make the bonds of Christ's love upon us even more secure and binding.

Nor angels, nor principalities, nor powers: No person or thing in any part of God's creation can break the Saviour's hold on the believer. Any such effort will but drive the trusting soul all the more dependently to the Saviour.

Nor any other creature: The great apostle has run the whole gamut and has exhausted every possibility of harm for the believer. He always comes back to the thrilling pronouncement that nothing anywhere can sever the golden chain that binds the heart of God to His people.

Which is in Christ Jesus our Lord: Earth has never known anything like the love of God. It is too big, too strong, too deep, too high, too wide, too pure, too marvelous for words or even thoughts to compass. You are in the middle of that love. You are precious in God's holy eyes. You are the one Christ died to save. You are the one He has commissioned the Holy Spirit to inhabit. Do these things pull on your heart? "Behold, what manner of love the Father hath bestowed upon us, that we should be called the sons of God. . . . And every man that hath this hope in him purifieth himself, even as he is pure" (1 John 3:1,3).

The challenge is still thrown down to us to walk triumphantly as we are led by the Holy Spirit. All the way through this great chapter Paul has assured us of the possibility of victorious living. He has been equally positive in telling us that we are obligated to live that holy life.

Why should we not live victorious lives? Why should we not follow in the footsteps of the One who has given us the supreme example of living above self and earthly desires? He has given us the example; we who believe have been called, justified, and glorified; and no power in all the universe can separate us from the power and love of God. Let us determine that our lives shall be nothing less than worthy of our calling.

> Fear not, I am with thee; O be not dismayed,
> For I am thy God, and will still give thee aid;
> I'll strengthen thee, help thee, and cause thee to stand,
> Upheld by my righteous, omnipotent hand.
>
> When through fiery trials thy pathway shall lie,
> My grace, all-sufficient, shall be thy supply:

The flame shall not hurt thee; I only design
Thy dross to consume, and thy gold to refine.

The soul that on Jesus hath leaned for repose
I will not, I will not desert to his foes;
That soul, though all hell should endeavor to shake,
I'll never, no, never, no, never forsake!

ANONYMOUS

First Peter I

Blessed be the God and Father of our Lord Jesus Christ, which according to his abundant mercy hath begotten us again unto a lively hope by the resurrection of Jesus Christ from the dead, to an inheritance incorruptible, and undefiled, and that fadeth not away, reserved in heaven for you, who are kept by the power of God through faith unto salvation ready to be revealed in the last time. . . .

Wherefore gird up the loins of your mind, be sober, and hope to the end for the grace that is being brought unto you at the revelation of Jesus Christ; as obedient children, not fashioning yourselves according to the former lusts in your ignorance: but as he who has called you is holy, so be ye holy in all manner of conversation. . . .

Forasmuch as ye know that ye were not redeemed with corruptible things, as silver and gold . . . but with the precious blood of Christ, as of a lamb without blemish and without spot: who verily was foreordained before the foundation of the world, but was manifest in these last times for you. . . . See that ye love one another with a pure heart fervently.

II

Wherefore laying aside all malice, and all guile, and hypocrisies, and envies, and all evil speakings, as newborn babes, desire the sincere milk of the word, that ye may grow thereby.

X. Kept by the Power of God

PICTURE AN OLD APOSTLE in Rome, saddened by the martyrdoms of James, the Lord's brother, and Paul, the mighty interpreter of the gospel. Storm clouds are hovering over all of the Jewish and Christian world. Persecution is already showing its ugly head. The worst fury of Nero's awful blast is about to break on defenseless Christians in every part of the Empire. It is dangerous to be associated with the despised sect known as Christians. Peter is strangely stirred. What can he do to help the believers throughout the land?

Peter feels led by the Holy Spirit to write to the followers of Christ to bring strength and encouragement to them. Sylvanus (Silas), who had spent much time with Paul in his missionary labors, is with Peter in Rome and is unusually well prepared to write the letter. What is to hinder him?

We must realize that thirty years have passed since that morning of the resurrection. Peter has come a long way and has learned more than we can estimate. He has walked humbly, trustingly, and obediently with his Lord. He has lived over those unforgettable experiences so many times that every one of them is clear and distinct in his mind. The messages Jesus spoke have been brought back to his mind so that they can be repeated word for word.

The "big fisherman" has been led daily into a deeper understanding of the eternal truths of the gospel. He has been exceedingly active in preaching, teaching, and spreading the gospel. He has had much time alone with John Mark and has made it possible for Mark's Gospel to be written. In a very real sense, he is prepared in mind and heart and personal influence to write a strengthening letter to the persecuted Christians of the Roman world. They need the lift that will come from the doctrinal and practical messages from the pen of their great leader.

We turn to these stirring words with eagerness and anticipation. We pray that the Holy Spirit may lead us as He led Simon Peter in the long ago. The people of our day need this intensely practical message. It should bring to us a new hope, a new strength, a new confidence, a new quietness of mind, a new vision of glory, and a new sense of the presence of the Holy Spirit in our lives. We will be thrilled by Peter's daring assurances as he tells us of the promises of God, of an eternal inheritance, of salvation to be completed, and of the indescribable glory that is to be revealed. We will grow to be better Christians, more ardent followers of our Lord, and more faithful witnesses. May all these treasures be ours in this study.

Strangers . . . scattered . . . picked out ones (1–2): Peter writes to a multitude of very ordinary people who are privileged, under God, to be settled in pagan lands alongside unsaved people. These strangers are Christians who are a long way from home, living next door to and working with men and women who need the gospel. These neighbors will be watching them, learning from them, constantly present as living prospects. Part of the missionary program of God is to have scattered Christians living close by those who need the gospel message. Peter wants these lonely, frightened, discouraged Christians to be encouraged and challenged by this truth.

The *elect* are the "picked out ones." The adjective can mean "chosen," "picked out," or "selected." Again the sacred writer is pointing a special appeal to very ordinary people. He assures them that God has selected them.

Father . . . Spirit . . . Jesus Christ (2): Peter knows the Trinity. From his Lord and Saviour he has learned this distinct and simple doctrine. The Father chose these special witnesses. The Holy Spirit exerted His power over them and brought them to the Saviour. The Son, Jesus Christ, cleansed them in His own precious blood and consecrated them for sacred service.

Each saved individual has experienced such divine activity. That miracle has brought about a set of new men and new women who have been selected, brought, forgiven, cleansed, and consecrated. Now they find themselves on active duty in divinely chosen places to carry out the will of the Father, under the direction and encouragement of the Holy Spirit. How could they regard themselves as of no account? How could they imagine their lives forgotten by the Father? They are special creations, selected, sanctified, saved, and commissioned. They must carry on for their Lord through every hour of trial or suffering. Their faith will increase as they walk with the Holy Spirit and see the victories He wins in and through them.

Obedience (2): The election of a Christian is election *unto obedience*. When will we learn that simple truth? When will Christians return to that fundamental concept and forget the idea that election is to some high honor, privilege, or position? The Scriptures always stress, just as Peter does

in this verse, the real end of God's choice. It is always to
obedience. The elect must obey Christ. All life long they
are to walk according to the will of their Lord. Nothing less
than full obedience can be considered.

Grace . . . peace (2): In his meaningful word of greeting Peter uses a combination of Christian and Hebrew saluta-
tions. The greeting adopted by Christians who spoke Greek
was *charis,* "grace." The salutation used by the Jews was
shalom, "peace." These were well-established greetings.
Peter greets those to whom he writes by saying, *Grace unto
you, and peace, be multiplied.* He is aware of the aim of
the Holy Spirit to bring Gentiles and Jews together in a
Holy fellowship, so he combines the two common saluta-
tions into a special Christian greeting. It is a joyous word
of lift and encouragement to all.

DOCTRINAL SECTION (3–12)

Blessed (3): Peter begins with a high note of praise.
Paul has opened his epistles in this same manner. It is a
beautiful way to start. We must remember that the Christians
to whom Peter is writing are greatly agitated and depressed
by an oppressive sense of insecurity and imminent danger.
There is ample reason for alarm. Danger and destruction
and death loom before them. Nero is ready to launch his
cruel persecution. The real purpose of the epistle is to con-
firm the weak believers. To do this, Peter pours forth praise
to God. The word translated "blessed" is from the root from
which we get our words "eulogy" and "eulogize," and literally means "to speak well of."

The God and Father of our Lord Jesus Christ (3): Peter
wants it clearly understood that Jesus was both human and
divine. He had known the Lord both as a man praying to

the Father and as God himself. The humanity and deity of Jesus stand out.

Who hath begotten us (3): Peter also wants to record his everlasting debt to the Father God who had made him alive in Jesus Christ. The decisive moment of all moments was the Lord's resurrection from the dead. He came forth from among the dead bodies to stand in the bright light of the first Easter morning. That was the day of victory. Peter pauses to register his burst of praise to the Father, who made life possible through Christ.

Unto a lively hope (3): Peter goes back to his life with Jesus when all his hope had been built on the flimsy foundation of the triumph of an earthly kingdom. The cruel crucifixion had dashed all his hopes and left him in utter despair. How dark that night of despair! Then Jesus came forth from the grave and a new and living (lively) hope was born within him, God's glorious gift to the despondent disciple. Peter remembers and pauses to shout his praises to the one who had caused that lively hope to come alive in his heart.

Paul had described the men of Ephesus as having no hope. What a tragic situation! Could any picture be worse? The Greek and Roman civilizations could boast of power, wealth, culture, poetry, and philosophy, but no hope. Sophocles, at the peak of his popularity and prosperity, gave to the feeling of his time: "Not to be born at all—that is by far the best fortune: the second best is as soon as one is born with all speed to return thither whence one has come." Can you imagine such despair? C. E. B. Cranfield has said of that age: "Over that classical civilization death reigned as king of terrors, spoiling men's enjoyment of the present with the intruding thought of the future, so that life could seem a gift not worth receiving, and death in infancy preferable to growing up to the conscious anticipation of having to die." [1] Into this background came the lively or living hope based on the resurrection of our Lord Jesus Christ. Jesus was able to put the king of terrors off the throne forever. The resurrection gave birth to the living hope, and that hope gave a new dimension to life. Christians became men of hope because Jesus lives! We too shall live through faith in Him.

To an inheritance (4): Listen to the apostle as he pauses for a moment on such words as "hope," "salvation," "joy," "an inheritance," "rejoice," "kept," "power of God," "faith," "holy," "fear," "redeemed," "love one another," "newborn babes," "milk of the word," "that ye may grow." Do these images whet your appetite? Do they lure you on to walk with Peter as he opens to us the treasures found in Christ Jesus? Are you personally interested in going on with him to see the wonders of Christ's glory? Let us walk reverently as the Holy Spirit interprets for us.

The inheritance is a matchless concept. All through the Old Testament there was the teaching that the nation Israel was an elect people. The nation was chosen; the covenant was with Israel. In the New Testament we see our *high calling in Christ Jesus*—each of us, personally and individually, redeemed by His blood. Instead of an inheritance of land, our inheritance is in Him and we are God's inheritance.

Peter describes our inheritance as incorruptible, undefiled, nonfading, and reserved in heaven. What more could be said to make us rejoice in the remarkable treasure we have awaiting us? The Greek word translated "reserved" suggests constant watchfulness. Many of us will never have an inheritance of much value here in this world, as Peter's readers could not expect an earthly inheritance. The apostle assured

---

[1] *The First Epistle of Peter* (London: Northumberland Press, 1950), p. 23.

them that the most valuable inheritance ever prepared is truly theirs. Nothing can ravage or destroy it. No fault, no weakness, no flaw can ever be found in it. Age will not cause it to fade or lose its value or its precious qualities. It is actually "laid up" with their names on it in heaven's safety deposit box. Nothing in time or in eternity can interfere in any way with it or with their claim on it. That sublime inheritance is to be ready at the return of the Lord. It is their treasure. It is God's gift. Even the slave in Asia Minor could claim it. It will be an eternal possession. The Lord Jesus Himself has promised it.

Kept [garrisoned] *by the power of God* (5): Peter rises even higher when he assures the saints that each one of them is being constantly "garrisoned" (a military team) day and night by the power of God. What more could anyone ask? (Cf. Phil. 4:7.) During the fearful days of the World War II, when men and ammunition and supplies had to be transported through fields of enemy submarines and mines, the military leaders placed about these supply and troopships a circle of powerful fighting ships. They were convoyed all the way across the ocean. For many miles an umbrella of air power flew overhead. There was no other way to make the journey safely. Peter uses much the same figure to reveal the loving arm of our God who "garrisons" us all the way. The journey is safe with His great arms about us (Deut. 33:27).

Has it occurred to you that the precious inheritance is being safely kept by the Father's strong hand and that you, too, are being safely kept, mile by mile, across the intervening days or years until that treasure is reached? God will not let it be lost or ravaged until you arrive. He is certain that you will arrive safely. It is His pleasure to guard both treasures. Peter did not mean that these Christians would be able to live (physically) through the bitter night of Nero's persecution. He did mean that their eternal souls would be kept "safe and sound" and uninjured.

Through faith unto salvation (5): The preacher assures us that while faith is man's side, the keeping is God's part. *Salvation* is the full sum of all that God has in store for us, the full enjoyment of our inheritance. It is the fulfilment of His "plan of the ages."

The Father wants all men to come into this salvation. He has provided grace enough for all. He loves with an unceasing love. The Lord Jesus died and made an atonement that is sufficient for all. The step of faith (simple personal trust in Christ) is one that any soul can easily and safely take. Salvation is the answer, the treasure, the eternal gift of God. God planned salvation. Christ came to die. The Holy Spirit came to quicken—all for you and for me. Our salvation is *ready to be revealed at the last time*. God has infinite riches in store for us. "Beloved, now are we the sons of God, and it doth not yet appear what we shall be: but we know that, when he shall appear, we shall be like him; for we shall see him as he is" (1 John 3:2).

Ye rejoice (6): Peter assured the believers that they had cause for genuine rejoicing. Their joy should be full, abiding, and unhindered. The *hope* he has described is to be realized in the future. Their joy is a part of the present, born of their new life in Christ. It is securely founded in their love for their Lord, in the salvation that is already theirs, in the constant presence and power of the Holy Spirit, in the wondrous hope of glad fulfilment over there, and in the heaven-sent privilege of witnessing to the grace of God. Nothing can stop their *great rejoicing*. (Cf. 1:8; 4:13.)

Manifold temptations . . . trial of your faith (6–7): At last Peter mentions the fiery trials that are breaking about the Christians. He has waited until he has reminded them of their great *inheritance,* their eternal *hope,* and the abiding *joys* that they possess. Against such a background, *temptations* and *trials* look smaller and less destructive. He assured them that they may expect tragic experiences along the way. The temptations and the fiery testings will only serve to bring out their faith and produce character that will stand the strain in every moment of suffering. The faith that comes through the fire will be more precious than the finest gold that has literally come through the fire of the refiner. The reference to gold would catch instant attention. Each slave reading these words would know of the frantic efforts to get gold coins to be used to purchase freedom from slavery. Peter assured them that the results of the trial of faith is more precious than all the gold in the land.

Precious (7) : It may be profitable to pause here to note Peter's use of this word "precious." In this verse *the trial of your faith is precious* because it brings out the love, grace, mercy, and resources of God. In 1:19 he speaks of *the precious blood of Christ,* and in 2:4 he describes "the living stone" as "precious." The Master is precious "unto you who believe" (2:7). In his second epistle Peter speaks of "precious faith" (1:1) , and of course in this present chapter he glories in the "exceeding great and precious promises." How wonderful to have a big, rough fisherman use such a delicate and beautiful word express the deep sense of abiding value attached to the treasures in Christ Jesus, his Lord. How exceedingly precious those treasures are! Our Lord is precious to us and will become increasingly so as we come to know Him through the fiery trials of life.

Look for a moment on the words of Napoleon, penned while he was in prison on St. Helena: "An extraordinary power of influencing and commanding men has been given to

cording to the outward behavior of the worldly pagans. These believers had come from a background that was distinctly pagan. No Christian, Jew or Gentile, has any business behaving as the pagans of that day did. The Lord Jesus is hidden completely in these men who prefer to cover Him with the clothing of heathenism. Have you left behind all evidences of your unregenerate past? Peter has a powerful word for you.

Be ye holy in all manner of living (15–16): Is Peter asking too much? Is the standard too high? Peter does not think it is. It is the same call that Jesus sounded in the Sermon on the Mount. He knew the weakness and the frailty of men, the power of the tempter, and the difficulties of living a holy life. In the light of all these things He still insisted that we must reach for the goal of holiness. Jesus has set the standard high. He supplies the power to reach it. It is God's will that, in every step of life's walk, the Christian should walk in the light of this goal. The word "conversation" (cf. Phil. 1:27) includes all the activity of the life— thoughts, words, deeds—and is properly translated "manner of life."

Father . . . fear (17): Peter is happy to find these believers calling God "Father." If they call God "Father," however, they must realize that they are drawing very close to God and must be conscious of His presence. They are using a privilege and resting in a choice relationship that should influence their attitude and conduct. They must "fear" in such relationship with the holy God. Reverence, awe, and humility must characterize them. They must be sensitive to the sort of response to be expected in His presence. They must, in the bright light about them, see and understand their own sins and sinfulness and beg forgiveness. They must, like children, love the Father so much that His wishes shall be interpreted as compelling commands. Intimate and sweet communion with Him will prove a blessing to their hearts.

You were redeemed . . . precious blood . . . lamb . . . the blood of Christ (18–20): Jesus had said, "The Son of man came not to be ministered unto, but to minister, and to give His life a ransom for many" (Mark 10:45). Peter reminds us that silver and gold coins did not buy redemption but that the biggest price that can be imagined was produced to ransom us from the dominion of sin and the devil. The ransom was the *precious blood of Christ*. This is true to the teachings of his great Teacher. A slave might buy his own ransom with silver and gold coins, but this slavery to sin could not be ended by producing all the coins in the Roman Empire. The price was the precious blood of the Son of God, heaven's gift to redeem human hearts and lives. Isaiah had said, "He was wounded for our transgressions, he was bruised for our iniquities: the chastisement of our peace was upon him; and with his stripes we are healed. All we like sheep have gone astray; each one has turned unto his own way; and the Lord hath laid on him the iniquity of us all" (53:5–6). Peter and Isaiah and Jesus agree.

Love one another with a pure heart fervently (22): Peter has just called these faithful ones "believers in God." Then, saying, "Seeing you have purified your souls in your obedience to the truth," he dares come to them with this beautiful demand. They have truly dedicated themselves to their beloved Redeemer and to an "unfeigned love of the brethren." Now is the time to give the world a great demonstration of human love in action. Here is the acid test. Do we love one another?

The root meaning of the word translated "fervent" has to do with stretching. Fervent love is a strenuous, active, persistent, and enduring love for the brethren. It is a genuine,

active, outgoing love that is plainly and unmistakably
discernible. No one can mistake it for something else or
something else for it. It follows the pattern lived out by
Christ. Look carefully and thoughtfully into the meaning of
John 3:16. Read John's powerful word in 1 John 4:7–21.
Can you ignore these words? The New Testament seeks to
make us love one another.

*Wherefore laying aside all malice . . . guile . . . hypoc-
risies . . . envies . . . evil speakings* (2:1): On the basis of
fervent love, Peter begins his definite call for a complete
renunciation of the old life. He urges these young converts
to refuse to carry over into their new lives their pagan traits,
habits, handicaps, and ungodly sins. He does not want them
bringing paganism into the life, ministry, and example of
the new Christian fellowship. A new life has been imparted.
A new life experience is demanded. Sin will not be allowed
in the new creatures in Christ. The "kingdom man" must
live on the higher plane.

Peter singles out five sins that are most tenacious. They
must be put out. *Malice* has in it the sort of ill will and
selfishness that seeks to hurt anyone it touches. *Guile* has to
do with deceit, treachery, and unfair dealings in business and
personal relations. *Hypocrisy* deals in pretense, play-acting,
covering one's identity, camouflage. Jesus used blistering
words to denounce the hypocrites. *Envy* is the worst. It has
poison in it. It begrudges the other person that which is
his. It is unspeakably ugly in God's sight. *Evil speakings* are
neither attractive nor desirable. Often the person who is
free to speak evil hurts innocent hearts and does the kingdom
a great deal of harm. Defaming, slandering, and hurting
others have no place in the colony of heaven. Christ does
not welcome such conduct.

As newborn babes, desire the sincere milk . . . grow

(2:2): Peter wanted these babes in Christ to grow. Why not? He declared that as Christians they must develop a strong yearning to make commendable growth. How can they satisfy their Lord or do the work assigned to them if they starve themselves and remain babies? The food on which they are to feed is the *sincere milk* of the word. It is unadulterated, unmixed, undiluted, and nourishing. It is God's prescription for positive growth. A Christian can find in God's Word the strong ingredients that fortify him for the development that makes him strong, healthy, and effective as a Christian witness.

May we find in Peter's vigorous words to the young saints of Asia Minor a strong challenge to our hearts. We will love our Lord, praise Him, tell others of Him, grow daily more like Him, pour out adoration and worship to Him, and dedicate our lives to help influence those among whom we live to come to Him for salvation and that eternal inheritance awaiting those who have committed their hearts to Him.

Ephesians IV

I . . . *beseech you that ye walk worthy of the vocation where-with ye are called, with all lowliness and meekness, with long-suffering, forbearing one another in love. . . . Till we all come in the unity of the faith, and of the knowledge of the Son of God, unto a perfect man, unto the measure of the stature of the fulness of Christ: that we . . . be no more children, tossed to and fro, and carried about with every wind of doctrine, . . . but speaking the truth in love, may grow up into him in all things, which is the head, even Christ. . . .*

That ye put off . . . the old man, which is corrupt according to the deceitful lusts; and be renewed in the spirit of your mind; and that ye put on the new man. . . . Wherefore putting away lying, speak every man truth with his neighbour. . . . Be ye angry, and sin not . . . neither give place to the devil. Let him that stole steal no more. . . . Let no corrupt communication proceed out of your mouth. . . . Grieve not the holy Spirit of God, whereby ye are sealed unto the day of redemption. . . . Be ye kind one to another, tenderhearted, forgiving one another, even as God for Christ's sake hath forgiven you.

V

Be ye therefore followers of God, as dear children; and walk in love, as Christ also hath loved us, and hath given himself for us an offering and a sacrifice to God.

XI. Walking Worthily

Ephesians IV

HOW IS A CHRISTIAN to live? How clean is his life to be? How thoughtful, trustful, honest, and dedicated to his Lord must he prove himself? Paul devoted three chapters of this epistle to the Ephesian Christians to the doctrinal and the spiritual aspects of redemption. He built up the finest statement of Christ's work in the atonement and the establishment of His church that can be found anywhere. Then he turned to a clear-cut treatment of the believer's response. He urges the individual to catch sight of his sublime privileges in Christ and to set out to live worthily as a member of the church. The great doctrines must be brought down to life, and a demonstration of their worth must be given as the Christian lives among the people of the world. He must exhibit a becoming life and wage a militant warfare against the kingdom of the devil. Chapters four, five, and six of this letter follow the doctrinal statement and are intensely practical. Let us seize them and let them make our lives victorious.

Walk worthily . . . the calling (1): The great apostle reminds his readers that he is a *prisoner of the Lord.* As he suffered for Christ's cause, Paul was able to give full proof of his sincerity, his loyalty, and his devotion to his Lord. His chains held him back from some of the activity he desired, but those chains preached eloquently day by day. The challenge thrown down to the Gentile Christians of Ephesus was that they walk as men should walk in the light of the calling extended by the Lord. How could they be content with ordinary lives? How could they stoop to sinful lives? Paul has no compromise ground for them. Their lives must be *worthy* (cf. Phil. 1:27; Col. 1:10; 1 Thess. 2:12). They had been called to enjoy God's free grace, to have a place in the select brotherhood of the redeemed, to exhibit daily the qualities and virtues of Christ, to help reach all men with the gospel message, and to share the wondrous joys of eternal glory. In the light of this calling, how could they do less than live worthy lives?

Lowliness . . . meekness . . . longsuffering . . . forbearing (2): If we are to demonstrate a worthy response, we must have spirits, dispositions, and hearts that make worthy conduct normal. *Lowliness* indicates that one has a modest opinion of his own abilities. It is a distinctive Christian grace. Paul sets it forth as utterly necessary. *Meekness* implies gentle submissiveness under trial. No resentment, no retaliation, no revenge is to be tolerated. Meekness requires strength. *Longsuffering* signifies patient endurance, a willingness and an ability to "stay under" the load in all circumstances. *Forbearing one another in love* speaks for itself. Love is active and beautiful. It found its most beautiful demonstration in Jesus of Nazareth. Love will do much in a life (1 Cor. 13:4–7).

Giving diligence to guard the unity of the Spirit (3): The worthy member of the church is one who is unceasingly eager to bring about full unity among the group. Many differing minds, backgrounds, and wills are present in the church. Constant striving will be needed to help the Holy Spirit maintain the peaceful behavior that makes for joyous growth and progress. Spiritual oneness can be achieved. The Holy Spirit can move forward in satisfactory strides when those of us who make up the church strive diligently toward this ideal.

One body . . . one God and Father (4–6): These verses present a powerful sevenfold ideal which serves as a secure foundation for the kind of unity Paul envisions. The *body* is the entire group of believers who become a part of it when they trust Christ for salvation. The *Spirit* is, of course, the Holy Spirit, who vitalizes, energizes, guides, and empowers those who make up the *body*. The *hope* is God's hope for the full consummation of His eternal plan of the ages for His saints. The *Lord* is the Son of God, who became the Babe of Bethlehem and died on Calvary to make atonement for our sins. He conquered sin and death and rose again to newness of life. He ascended to the Father to become Lord of lords and King of kings. He is the Prince and Possessor of all His people equally. One day He is coming again. The *faith* is the one simple believing experience which is common to all who are saved. This living experience of faith in Him as personal Saviour is our bond of unity. The *baptism* is our expression of our allegiance to Jesus Christ as Saviour and Lord. (Cf. Gal. 3:27; Rom. 6:1–11; Col. 2:12.) Men may, because of desire for convenience, adopt a different mode of baptism. They may even attach undue importance to the ordinance. But there is this possibility for agreement: for all Christians it is a solemn profession of faith in the risen Lord as personal Saviour. *One God* climaxes Paul's list. He is the Father of all believers. He thus becomes for us the ultimate source of spiritual unity. Father (v. 6), Son (v. 5), and Spirit (v. 4) combine in these verses to make a powerful appeal for the ideal unity in the *body*.

To each one of us the grace was given (7) : Paul puts a large responsibility upon each member of the group to keep the unity of the *body*. No one can escape the pressure. In order to assure full and effective participation, each one is equipped with a special portion of the grace of God, bestowed by Christ Himself. His plan is to make every believer adequate to contribute to the full work of the group. He knows exactly how much of His grace is needed by each new Christian.

Paul quotes from Psalm 68:18 to give an illustration of Christ's victorious capture of men and women as new trophies and as new members of His *body*. By means of Christ's work, the *body* is constantly enlarged and the kingdom is extended.

Apostles . . . prophets . . . evangelists . . . pastors and teachers (11): In this remarkable passage Paul describes the method the Master used in promoting the ends for which He had established the church. The emphasis is not upon orders or office. It is upon spiritual gifts designed to fit individuals to further the divine plans and to bring about the full growth and progress of Christ's cause on earth. The *apostles* were missionaries. They had to do with the establishment of the churches. The twelve made up the first list. Barnabas, Paul, Timothy, Silas, and others were later members of this group. In no sense were they clothed with unusual authority. They were commissioned to go with the gospel. The *prophets* were chosen and set apart as special agents of the Holy Spirit in guiding, directing, counseling, and leading the young churches in the larger areas. The *evangelists* were preachers of the gospel in new sections of the land. With zeal and fervor they made new converts to the cause of Christ. The *pastors* and *teachers* were shepherds of the flocks. Guidance and instruction were their assignments. They were permanent local leaders of organized congregations.

For the equipment of the saints . . . and the building up of the body of Christ (12): These new Christians were far from being strong church workers. They needed special training, teaching, counseling, encouraging, and fitting before they would be ready for active service. They were to be built solidly into the gathering of many new "living stones," and their incorporation into the working body of believers called for the best thinking, praying, and working the believers were capable of.

Unto a full-grown man . . . the fulness of Christ (13): What a goal Paul set for his friends at Ephesus! He will not be content *until we all arrive at the unity of the faith.* Nothing less can be worthy of Christians. Each member must grow and become mature until perfect manhood in Christ is attained. Each one will so relate himself to the *Head* (Christ) and to each member of the *body* (the church) that the measure of the stature of the fully grown Christ will be realized. Paul has caught the vision of the complete *body* nurtured daily by the Holy Spirit and the apostles, prophets, evangelists, pastors, and teachers. In time it will not only please Christ but actually make perfect the full meaning of the goal He has set for the kingdom. You are one of the individuals he would challenge to help attain this ideal. Are you making progress toward the goal? Is He satisfied with your growth in grace? What is your honest appraisal of your fitness, your willingness, your contribution?

No longer children (14): As we hold before our eyes the goal of verse thirteen—the fulness of Christ—we are cautioned to check up on our immaturity, our instability, our shallow understanding, and our undependability. Because of these glaring faults we hinder the work of the *body* and delay the progress of the entire group. The Holy Spirit prods and challenges, but we are hinderers. We feel quite a jolt when we are confronted with the charge that we are babes and that we ought to grow up. We need to be pulling our part of the load. Instead of demanding special care and correction and coddling, we need to be walking with buoyant stride in the very forefront of the marching company. When will we become mature? When can the Holy Spirit count on us for worthy participation?

But speaking the truth in love (15): Paul demanded that his friends grow up. He pointed them to the ideal of being true, loyal, devoted, faithful. Alford's translation of these words is "being followers of truth." They must know the truth, love it, speak it, and embody it in conduct. It is this prescription that will bring the Christian into the spirit that identifies him with the Head, for it is from Christ that growth is possible. From Him flows the vital supply that builds the mature man. In Him is found the essence of truth, holiness, and fulness of life. As each member grows up in Christ, the *body* grows into the fulness and likeness of the *Head.* Love is the ingredient that most perfectly identifies the member with his Lord and guarantees the growth that pleases Him. Love is to be taken in large doses. Jesus had a way of asking, "Lovest thou me?" (John 21:15–17).

Fitly framed and knit together . . . maketh increase (16): In this difficult passage the apostle uses the figure of the human body to illustrate the process of growth in the *body*. With perfect harmony of operation, with direct contact with the *Head,* and with perfect intercommunication of all the parts, the whole *body* makes full and rapid progress toward perfection.

The increase of the body unto the building up of itself in love. Thus the perfect church emerges through the full co-operation of all the parts. Nourishment, fellowship, guidance, encouragement, participation, and love contribute toward the joyous building of the structure which approximates the fulfilment of the divine plan of the ages. The Holy Spirit works in and through us.

No longer walk as the Gentiles (17): These Christians are new creatures in the Lord. They must dare to be different. Turn back to Ephesians 2:1–3, 12 and see Paul's picture of them before they were saved. He declares that they walked as men of the world, without regard for God or right or eternity. They dangled like puppets on the puppet strings of the devil. They satisfied the natural urges of the body and mind without restraint. They *were without Christ, without hope, without God in the world*. Some of these Ephesian converts were continuing to walk like Gentiles. No radical change had come about in their behavior. No one could recognize them as Christians. Paul is old-fashioned enough to hold that a great change comes over a person when he is born again. His thoughts, his words, his deeds, and his manner of life are all radically different.

In these verses Paul cuts straight through with clear language to bring the Ephesian Christians face to face with the Christian standard of living. There are certain principles that must find expression in daily life. Nothing short of strong, clean, victorious living can be acceptable to the Head of the *body*. Christians constitute a new type of humanity. By walk, by word, by witness they are different. Ethically and morally they are to demonstrate the new life. Standards are different. A marked difference must be maintained so that any neighbor can know immediately that Christ lives in them.

Christians are a "colony of heaven" set down in the midst of a heathen world. They are set down among the others to effect ethical and spiritual conquests in the earth. They make a formidable "beachhead" that is to be the vantage point for a vigorous offensive by the Christian forces. No victories can be won if their conduct is not distinctively different. Their lives are to be lived worthily of God's high calling in Christ Jesus. No heathen standard is high enough for a child of the King.

In the emptiness of their minds (17): How pitiful it is to see those unsaved people groping about in the insane folly of their minds, believing that sinful indulgence brings pleasure. Romans 1:18–32 gives us a graphic picture of these deluded creatures who moved further and further away from God as they sought blindly and foolishly to find pleasures that could satisfy their appetites and imaginations. How can one born in the image of God lose himself so completely? The apostle sought to stir the believers of Ephesus to come out from such vile conduct before they had disgraced the cause of Christ and hindered the *body* in its climb toward perfection. *In the madness of their minds* they will find themselves repeating the picture in Romans unless they turn and let the Holy Spirit direct their ways and love rule their hearts.

Having been darkened in the understanding (18): Since these people have been *alienated from God,* they find that their power of reasoning has failed them. Decay has set in. "Sin has cut the optic nerve of the soul" and moral distinctions cannot be made. Morally, mentally, and ethically they are diseased. Sin has a way of bringing such disease. Paul would save believers from it. He would save the church from such dangerous representatives.

Ignorance . . . hardness of heart . . . past feeling (18–

19): The pagans are morally stupid. They are totally ignorant of the truth about God, holiness, and salvation. This
ignorance is the real ground for the darkened understanding,
the hardness of heart, and the alienation from God. We do
not behave as Christians if we are wholly ignorant of the
things of God. Sins, excesses, and pagan practices can always
be counted on to take over in such minds. Paul urges the
believers to watch these tragic evidences of decay and estrangement from God. Ignorance and hardening of heart
brought about spiritual paralysis. No feeling whatever was
in evidence. Conscience refused to rise up and knock. These
people had "ceased to feel pain." They had gone so far that
they had lost moral sensitivity. They were utterly insensible
to truth, honor, shame, and spiritual impulses.

They gave over themselves (19): You can hardly find a
more tragic picture. How could life be worth living? What
did they have left? What did they have to lose? At any rate,
Paul says they took up what was left of their own precious
selves and deliberately and greedily gave it over to the lowest and vilest sorts of impurity, sexual vice, and unclean behavior. With reckless abandon they plunged into the vilest
behavior they could find. *Greediness* indicates a wild, eager,
passionate grasping after something that might gratify the
lusts and urges of depraved minds and bodies. Sensual vices,
gross licentiousness, inhuman practices, and Godless conduct
characterized those who had been innocent creations of God.
Such was Paul's picture of them.

But you did not so learn Christ (20): These new converts
had had a rich experience, and they had been taught by
good teachers. They knew Christ better than to attribute
such behavior to His choosing. They knew that it did not
please Him. They knew better than to unite a Gentile life
with a Christian profession. In the historical Jesus of Naza-

reth are embodied the true teachings, the true standards of
living, the true directions for Christian conduct. He lived
and taught that which was diametrically opposed to the conduct of the worldly Gentiles of Ephesus. He is to control
behavior and to set standards leading to purity of life and
devoted loyalty. The Holy Spirit is constantly near to teach,
to interpret, and to challenge us to the higher living demon-
strated by Christ Jesus.

Put off . . . be renewed . . . put on (22–24): The figure
is that of a man taking off an old garment and putting it
completely away in one single act of strong decision. That
act is the pattern for every person to follow when he becomes a Christian. The old garment was deliberately abandoned. There was to be no going back to it. No moment
of weakness could make right its being put on again. It was
corrupt and morally decaying; it could have no value, no
attractiveness. Why should a newborn believer want to bring
over into his new life the disease-laden garment of the old
life? Like an old shoe or hat it might be comfortable, but
the believer is a new creature and should not have any desire
for it.

A present infinitive (indicating gradual, continuous progress and growth) introduces the second idea, *Be renewed in
the spirit of your mind.* Notice that the form is passive, indicating that the renewing must come from the outside. The
Holy Spirit must do the renewing, but He waits for the individual to show willingness. It is most natural to expect the
mind to undergo a full renewal when the old garment has
been completely abandoned. The mind is ready and waiting
for the happy miracle to come. The verb "renewed" comes
from a root that means "become youthful." It is good to
know that the Holy Spirit stands ready to renew our minds.
The process is a continuous one as He works in us.

The third step in the schedule is to *put on the new man*. The picture was Paul's way of challenging the Gentiles to recognize their status as new creatures in Christ Jesus. (Cf. Rom. 13:14, in which we are told to *put on the Lord Jesus Christ*.) *Righteousness and holiness* will characterize the new man. Willing conformity to the law, plus the willingness to recognize and reverence everlasting sanctities, are to be found in the new child of the King. These two thoughts complete the idea of moral and ethical perfection. Righteousness speaks of the right conduct of a man toward his fellows, while holiness has to do with his conduct toward God. Holiness is the sum of moral perfection as it exists in God.

Putting away lying . . . speak [do] the truth (25): Pagan vices must be put aside. Christian virtues must be put in their place. *Being members one of another,* the believers must make this change. *Being in Christ,* the believer is in a rare air that demands the truth. This test applies not only to the words of his mouth but also to every phase of his life. Lying words, lying practices, and lying deeds must all be gone. They do not belong. The believer is in Christ. He is a new creature. Not one bit of false living can be in place. The Bible is unalterably opposed to any form of false representation. Paul is speaking on a high plane when he reminds his readers that the slightest weakening in the realm of honesty will seriously affect the whole *body*.

Be angry . . . do not sin (26): The Christian can have a full burst of righteous indignation against evil without sin. When anger comes in any other guise, it can very easily represent wounded personality or wronged pride. It is dangerous. Paul declares that the Christian must be in full control and never let anger break forth into sin. To suppress it, restrain it, overcome it, or dismiss it immediately as an unworthy guest is to keep from sinning. It is not Christlike to let anger take over and spoil a sweet disposition, embarrass friends, and grieve the Holy Spirit. Anger is wholly unnecessary, unavailing, and unbecoming. Yielding to anger gives the devil an opportunity to take over and cause serious trouble in the peace of the group. When he gains control, he delights to destroy the unity that is in Christ.

Let him that stole no longer steal (28): Stealing is an ugly habit. It is unchristian. It disturbs the peace. It displeases our Lord. Why steal? Do you know a thief? Perhaps he conducts a business by dishonest methods or exacts too much interest or rent or too big a price. Perhaps he has his own ways of taking that which does not belong to him. Whatever those ways are, Paul is against them. The Gentile world may not see any harm in them, but the New Testament is against them. The apostle suggests that we go to work with our own hands and acquire our money honestly.

Let no foul speech come from your mouth (29): How do you measure up here? The adjective "foul" literally means "rotten," "putrid," or "foul smelling." Do you want anything like that to come pouring out of your mouth? We are strongly urged to understand that such language does not fit a Christian's mouth. Whether profanity, vulgar stories, rotten language, hurtful gossip, or worthless chatter, it is hurtful to our Lord's cause and must hurt His great heart. How can a Christian forget himself so completely as to dishonor the Master in such a way?

For edifying of the need (29): The other side of the picture is beautifully presented. How the soul needs building! This verse reminds us of need here, there, and yonder. Hearts are down, spirits are depressed, discouragement looms. How is a member of the sacred family circle going to respond? Paul suggests that good words may be spoken at the right moment, in the right tone of voice, with a sincere

prayer. Eternity alone will reveal the tremendous blessing
that comes to the heart thus spoken to. An encouraging word
may be worth more than can ever be known. We are assured
that the Christian may *minister grace* to the needy heart.
What a striking contrast with the idea of foul speech! Paul
claims that the Christian will have in his heart the desire to
refrain from the one and be led by the Holy Spirit to the
other. It is up to you.

Grieve not the Holy Spirit (30): Would you know when
you grieve Him? The word means to "make sorrowful,"
"disturb," "distress," "hurt," "offend." Maybe the verses we
have been reading will throw some light on the answer to
the question. Can you honestly think of some everyday deeds
that will grieve Him? Remember that He is constantly with
us. He knows what we think, what we say, what we do. No
thought, no word, no deed escapes Him. Would you be
happy in the thought that you have offended Him or grieved
Him today? Paul reminds us that it was He who sealed us
when we were born again. The seal of God's ownership of
us was put upon us by the Holy Spirit. If we are Christians
we will seek diligently to think and say and do the things
that will be pleasing to Him. We belong to the Lord. He
lives in us.

*Bitterness . . . wrath . . . anger . . . clamor . . . evil
speaking . . . malice . . . put away* (31): Dr. E. Y. Mullins
has given us a helpful paragraph on these words:

Verse 31 enumerates another group of sins which also are opposed to the ideal unity of the body of Christ. They [Christians]
are commanded to put away "bitterness" which means a resentful
disposition and inward hardness of spirit toward others; "wrath"
which means the excited state which follows the undue indulgence of the bitter feeling; "anger," or the more settled attitude
which often remains after the outbreak of wrath; "clamor," or

the loud outbursts of anger; "railing," which means reviling, the deliberate utterance of hurtful things against another which may succeed the clamor. All these are to be put away. . . . Malice is a state of mind closely resembling the bitterness or resentment mentioned first, but is rather more deeply seated. Malice is a sin which results from an inherently evil disposition, while bitterness or resentment is the result of some occasion which excites it. The best definition of malice is to consider it as opposed in all respects to the graces which are enumerated in the next verse.[1]

Be ye kind . . . tenderhearted . . . forgiving (32): Paul does not lay down stern prohibitions without an appeal to positive goodness. The word "kind" first meant "useful," then "helpful," then "kind." Kindness is opposed to bitterness and selfishness. How it is needed in the world! Throughout the world men who are kind are bringing hope and cheer to weary hearts. Homes are transformed. Joy, gladness, and gratitude are in evidence. Kindness is truly a Christian virtue. The apostle urges Christians to become *kind*. *Tenderhearted* individuals are ready to be kind openly. Considerateness is a sorely needed quality of soul.

Forgiveness is a divine prerogative, and a forgiving soul becomes an instrument of grace. The Heavenly Father set the pattern for all forgiveness. We are to act *even as God in Christ made himself gracious to you*. Since we are in Christ, we must behave even as our Father did in this matter of forgiveness. Our Lord taught forgiveness by word and deed all through His earthly life. He looks for it in us every day of our lives. He makes it a vital part of the demands made upon those who have accepted His forgiveness (Matt. 6:14–15; Mark 11:26).

Become therefore imitators of God . . . walk in love

---

[1] *Studies in Ephesians and Colossians* (Nashville: Sunday School Board, Southern Baptist Convention, 1913), pp. 73–74.

. . . as also Christ loved us, and delivered himself up for us an offering and a sacrifice to God (5:1): This verse forms a beautiful climax of Paul's appeal to believers to *walk worthily of the calling.* Christians are to be *imitators of God!* In the hard going of the busy life we are lifted by the challenge to set as our life's goal the imitation of God. The prescription is given—*walk in love.*

Paul believed that Christians could walk in love—even in Ephesus. He let them understand that they have an obligation to live in line with that ideal. Living in love will make the difference. It will be possible only as love fills hearts and minds and lives. A life of love will be a powerful and victorious life. It will call out the best within us. We can "mount up with wings as eagles," we can "run and not be weary," we can "walk and not faint." We will shout with Paul, "We are more than conquerors through him that loved us" (Rom. 8:37).

Christ gave us the supreme example of love in His becoming an offering and a sacrifice to pay the price for our redemption. His atoning death made eternal life possible for everyone who trusts in Him. His sacrificial love for us will constantly challenge us to love Him and to love the other members of the sacred *body* of which He is the *Head.*

Philippians I

I thank my God upon every remembrance of you, . . . being confident . . . that he which hath begun a good work in you will perform it until the day of Jesus Christ. . . . And this I pray, that your love may abound yet more and more in knowledge and in all judgment; that ye may approve things that are excellent; that ye may be sincere and without offence till the day of Christ; being filled with the fruits of righteousness, which are by Jesus Christ, unto the glory and praise of God. . . .

For to me to live is Christ, and to die is gain. . . . Only let your conversation be as it becometh the gospel of Christ: that . . . I may hear of your affairs, that ye stand fast in one spirit, with one mind striving together for the faith of the gospel; and in nothing terrified by your adversaries . . . but to you of salvation, and that of God. For unto you it is given in the behalf of Christ, not only to believe on him, but also to suffer for his sake; having the same conflict which ye saw in me, and now hear to be in me.

XII. The Changeless Challenge

Philippians I

IT IS BEAUTIFUL to see the love of a pastor for his flock. It is even more beautiful to see the people give evidence of their love for the pastor. Ten years had passed since Paul and his three companions had attended the prayer meeting by the side of the river in Philippi. Out of that service had grown Paul's favorite church. Lydia had proved to be a tower of strength for the little band of believers. The jail experience had given a powerful impetus to the work. Paul and Silas, with bleeding backs, had preached and prayed and sung the message of the gospel throughout the reaches of the old jail. The Holy Spirit had given a mighty victory in Philippi. A Jewish woman, a Greek girl, and a Roman jailer had formed a good beginning for the church.

The ten years had rolled by swiftly. Twice Paul had visited his friends in Philippi. A strong love had continued to grow in the hearts of preacher and people. For four years they had not seen each other. Paul had been in prison the greater part of that time. These friends prayed for him constantly and their love for him grew. Recently Epaphroditus had made the long journey, bringing to Paul assurance of love, concern, and appreciation. Along with supplies, delicacies, and much-needed articles of clothing, they sent him money to help ease his burdens and provide funds to carry on his work. This expression of sincere love called for the response we have in the precious letter before us. It is literally steeped in appreciation and affection.

We need to remember that Paul was in prison, chained to a Roman soldier. He was seeking day and night to preach the gospel, writing letters to the churches, and constantly praying for the groups of Christians in Asia and Europe who had been led to Christ through his efforts. During this imprisonment he wrote to the Ephesians and the Colossians and to Philemon. Now he was dictating this beautiful letter to the Philippians. Timothy was with him. The Roman soldier sat by his side. Epaphroditus waited patiently to take the letter to his friends at Philippi. The members of that church continued to pray and wait for the return of Epaphroditus with Paul's word. The Holy Spirit was ready to pour into the mind of the great apostle the message for the church and the churches. It was probably the spring of A.D. 62.

GREETINGS (1-2)

Paul begins by declaring that he and Timothy regard themselves as *slaves of Christ Jesus*. He recognizes himself as being in the absolute possession of his redeeming Lord. He is not only working for and helping Christ, he is the property of Christ. He has been bought and has no rights whatever outside of the will of the Master. He had already said, "Ye are not your own. . . . Ye are bought with a price: therefore glorify God in your body, and in your spirit, which are God's" (1 Cor. 6:19-20). It is Christ's absolute ownership that is stressed.

Saints (holy ones): As purchased ones, the Philippian

Christians, too, are slaves of Christ. They are consecrated (separated) to Him, divinely set aside to sacred use. They are "holy ones" united in sacred relationship to the Holy One. It is a peculiar honor to be among that select group. As Christians they are to walk among the people of pagan Philippi bearing their witness in such a manner that all will recognize them as holy ones.

Grace . . . peace (2): Instead of the usual greeting, the great apostle writes a fervent prayer, using the Christian word "grace" and adding the Greek equivalent of the Hebrew *shalom,* "peace." Included in these two words is a picture of God's only remedy for sin and His prescription for full peace of mind and heart. God's love, kindness, and mercy all find their expression from this fountain of grace. There is no peace until grace has come. Christ is the only source of grace, the full answer to the quest for peace of mind. From his own experience Paul knows too well the groping, the confusion, the turmoil, the endless seeking for peace and soul satisfaction. He knows the unspeakable joy that came to him on the Damascus road when he opened his heart and let Christ come in.

THANKSGIVING AND PRAYER (3–11)

Praise, petition, and thanksgiving are all a part of the genuine prayer of the old pastor. He talks to God as he writes his people. His prayer abounds in praise, in faith, in love, in sincere appreciation, and in fervent petition.

I thank my God (3): Paul remembers the Philippian church, and as he does, his heart pours out praise and thanksgiving. He begins counting his blessings. Each beautiful deed, each sweet thoughtfulness, and each gracious kindness remind him of the love that is too precious for words. He begins thanking God.

Paul's life had been signally blessed by these devoted saints. Do we thank God sufficiently for human love, sympathy, understanding, and encouragement? We have no way of evaluating their impact on the life and work of a minister. Eternity alone will reveal the blessings that have come to hungry hearts through the years as thoughtful friends have made their Christian contribution. Paul says that the full remembrance of these expressions of love overwhelms him and sends him to the Father with thanksgiving and praise. Can one say that about you? Does the memory of all your deeds and words lead your pastor to a prayer of thanksgiving? Is that pastor so sensitive to a multitude of kindnesses that he turns heartily to praise God? Paul was unusually sensitive to loving thoughts, words, and deeds. May his tribe increase!

Request . . . on behalf of you . . . joy (4): Every time he thinks of his friends in Philippi, Paul prays, and when prayer begins, his heart overflows with joy. Having the great man of God lifting them in special prayer over and over again was a treasure too rich for words. Does someone pray for you? You would probably be surprised to know the number of special prayers that go up to the Father for you every day. Do you pray personally and individually for others? It is your privilege. Why not experience the joy of intercessory prayer? Samuel said, "God forbid that I should sin against the Lord in ceasing to pray for you" (1 Sam. 12:23). In James' epistle we read, "Ye have not, because ye ask not" (4:2). For ten years Paul has found peculiar *joy* in praying for his friends in Philippi. His soul lights up with true happiness when he prays for them.

Fellowship toward the gospel (5): The Philippian Christians' participation in the spread of the gospel is a thing of beauty and a cause for genuine thanksgiving. Paul is proud of them and wants them to visualize the good they have accomplished as his partners in spreading the gospel. Such a partnership has meant much in sending the message throughout the earth. Their giving has helped. Their sympathy and encouragement, their earnest participation in causing the church to grow and be strong, and their wholehearted love for the cause of the Christ have all been a great help to the apostle and to the work. Church members mean more to the ongoing of the work than they realize. Paul had received many blessings that helped him personally, but he was most delighted with the impetus these gifts had given to the cause of Christ.

He who initiated . . . will bring to perfection (6): Another reason for thanksgiving is Paul's confidence in the future. The past had brought joy, but the days ahead are even brighter for his beloved people in Philippi. The One who had begun the good work of salvation will see it through to its fullest completion. The supreme Author of the work of grace will guarantee rich fulfilment, for He is not one to begin something He cannot finish. Even until the coming of Christ, the work is to grow and prosper. God is faithful! "Lo, I am with you alway" (Matt. 28:20). Victory is assured.

I have you in my heart . . . my bonds . . . partakers of my grace (7): The preacher opens his heart again and lets his friends see that they are written on the inner places of his great heart. He is happy to hold them there as sharers of the grace entrusted to him. They have been co-partners with him in enjoying and passing on the heaven-sent message. They have had their part in the ministry of interceding, in the ministry of giving, and in the ministry of encouraging. They have been able to share with him the *bonds* that have caused him sore distress and cost opportunities for witnessing. In verse eight he breaks down and tells them of his intense longing to see them that is strangely like homesickness. He needs what they can give him. It is out of a powerful heart-hunger that this prayer comes.

I pray that your love may abound (9): Paul knows these friends and understands their needs. His first petition is that *love* may grow and overflow and increase until they will be surrounded by it and characterized by it. Their whole lives will be made strangely different. Paul's use of *agape* would seem to indicate love in its higher and broader sense. Hearts and minds are to be so full of love that every contact with an individual will reveal an overflowing demonstration of Christlike love. Paul has already described for the saints at Corinth the behavior of love (1 Cor. 13:4–7). He wanted his friends at Philippi to show even more the power of love.

Knowledge (9): Paul uses the word for knowledge that is reserved for the highest, the most fully developed, the most perfect knowledge. He wanted the believers at Philippi to develop the sort of knowledge that would make their strong love behave properly and wisely. They must have a thirst for knowledge that will make them seek it, search for it, find it, lay hold on it, and store it wisely so that it can be available for the working of the Master's will. Knowledge is power! How powerful are you? How much knowledge is stored in your brain? How well have you mastered the Word of God? The apostle would have you become a complete master of the wondrous truths of God's Book.

Discernment (9): It is not enough to have *knowledge*. The powerful Christian needs the power of discerning, perceiving, weighing relative values, reaching decisions, and becoming certain of the spiritual choice that results in victory. Good, keen, clear common sense and stable thinking will be valuable. The Christian must be able to know instinctively what matters and what is insignificant. Paul is praying that his friends in the old church might be able to make decisions that will please the Saviour. What more significant prayer could be prayed for you and for your people? *Love* will provide the ingredient that will contribute to this power of discernment. It is only in a flood of love that one is able to understand another's motives, actions, and inner spirit. Love is most potent when it pours itself out in knowledge and discernment. A keen, discerning Christian with a good store of knowledge and a heart full of love becomes a tremendous person in Christ's army. How well do you measure up?

Approve the things that are excellent (10): Paul prayed that those to whom he wrote might have positive discrimination. He prayed fervently that when *love* has opened the way, *knowledge* has made its contribution, and keen *discernment* has arrived at a decision, these Christians might have the courage to choose the high road and to act on that choice. It takes a powerful person to do that difficult deed. So many people can arrive at a good conclusion but cannot go through with the right action on that decision. The Greek words might be translated "the things that surpass" or "the things that differ," rather than "the things that are excellent." You use all your *knowledge* (heaped upon heap). You arrive at the wise decision through keen *discernment*. You test and approve and then commit yourself unreservedly to carrying out that which is high and holy and *excellent*. You have a sense of that which is vital and are able to act on the strong decision (Rom. 2:18). How do you rate yourself on this rung of the ladder? Do you always find yourself doing the things you have decided are right? Do you dare to be different for Christ's sake?

That you may be sincere and void of offence (10): Paul now prays that the use of *knowledge* and *discrimination* may result in a freedom from stain and offence, from stumbling or causing to stumble. He is concerned that character be built. He would have his readers progress to the point that they would have nothing in their words or thoughts or lives that would cause another to stumble or that would offend anyone. He wants them to be spotless in the sight of God and harmless in the sight of men. Are you reasonably sure that you are void of offence? Can you claim to be sincere, unsullied, unadulterated? Paul would pray as earnestly for you as for the Philippians. In a day when people are taught to be careful lest they offend friends and associates, it will be good for us to take special care to keep from offending God.

Being filled with the fruit of righteousness (11): Paul is fast approaching the climax of his special prayer for his Philippian friends. He dares pray, in the light of the coming day of Christ, that they be as full of the *fruit of righteousness* as they have been filled to overflowing with love. He wants to see an abundance of the fruit that righteousness produces ready for the day of Christ. Christ expects fruit from every Christian. Are you concerned that there be much of the fruit that springs from righteousness already heaped up when Jesus comes? We can meet Him with great heaps of this choice fruit. Christian living has two sides, character and the fruit of character. Paul prayed that the Philippian Christians might produce the finest fruit.

By Jesus Christ (11): Then the apostle hastened to pray that the saints at Philippi will not suppose that they can bring this fruit by their own power. *Jesus Christ* gives the power. He makes fruit possible. He said, "The branch cannot bear fruit of itself, except it abide in the vine; no more can ye, except ye abide in me" (John 15:4).

Unto the glory and praise of God (11): Just as Jesus insisted that the glory must be for His Father, Paul, in his prayer, begs that all glory and praise be for the Father. Jesus had said, "Herein is my Father glorified, that ye bear much fruit; so shall ye be my disciples" (John 15:8). Grace is never to terminate in individuals or in a church, but in the final working out of the Father's plan of the ages that men may stand before His throne in eternal praise.

In his prayer Paul asked for abounding love, a thirst for knowledge, a keen discernment, a courageous discrimination, and a fully developed character. All these things are to be used to heap up praise and glory to the eternal Father in heaven. That prayer is being offered up to Him for you now. Does it challenge you to help bring about its answer? It may be late, but it is not too late. Let the love of God flow through you and produce the graces that will make you beautiful.

THE GOSPEL'S PROGRESS (12–20)

Paul is determined to tell his friends how the work is advancing in Rome. In the midst of references to imprisonment and guards and opposition, he refers to the gospel and its progress more often than anything else. The soldiers who guard him know that he is a prisoner for the sake of the gospel of Jesus Christ. Each one who has come from the palace guard has gone away with the new truths of Christ ringing in his ears. One by one, these Roman soldiers are being brought face to face with the Saviour. Even Paul's chains are preaching eloquently.

The Christians of Rome have felt the impact of Paul's presence in their city. They have been encouraged, challenged, and quickened to be more active as Christians. They have gained courage to speak the words of the gospel with conviction and with power. They now dare to comfort men with the gospel. The gospel has come alive all over Rome because these brethren in Christ are preaching and witnessing with renewed enthusiasm.

Some of the believers in Rome, the Judaizers and the ones who stand with them, are troubling Paul. They cannot give Paul any encouragement or preach the gospel according to his interpretation. They insist on requirements that are not truly Christian. But they are preaching enthusiastically, and souls are being saved. The great apostle expresses himself as being pleased because *Christ is being proclaimed*. All his care is for *the progress of the gospel*. His joy is complete.

Paul is exceedingly happy that he can say, *Christ shall be magnified in my body, whether it be by life, or by death*. Every sentence he writes tells of this spirit. All he hoped or dreamed or sought was that he might focus the attention of others upon the lovely Saviour who meant more to him than all else in all the world. Paul's one consuming desire was that he might clear away everything so that others might see Jesus in all His purity, beauty, and glory. In these long hours of imprisonment, suffering, and loneliness *Christ is being proclaimed*. That is the victory. There is no bitterness, no self-pity, no complaining, no regrets; instead, there is abounding joy. His joy is to continue. New victories are to be won. The triumph of his faith is clearly assured.

DEATH OR LIFE (21-26)

Paul begins this discussion with his marvelous statement *to me to live is Christ*. For him life means Christ. No life is worth calling "life" except that which is spent with Christ. Christ is the aim, the very essence, the full reward of living. For Paul Christ is the sum of living. His supreme interest in life is Christ and His gospel. Nothing else matters at all. No other consideration enters into decisions concerning life and death. Christ has been the one theme of his preaching, the outpouring song of his heart, the goal of all his struggles, the one object of his adoration, the beloved Saviour who claimed every single interest of his soul, mind, and body. Living is Christ and dying is gain.

Thus is explained the statement *to die is gain*. Death merely means more of Christ and, for Paul, more of real living. He is certain that what we call death is but the entrance, immediately, into the very presence of Christ (2 Cor. 5:1). The doctrine of an intermediate state of sleep or an unconscious existence was not held by Paul. Paul knows that he will gain, either by dying or by continuing to live in the flesh. To be with Christ, to know Him better, and to feel the blessedness of His presence will be a rich treasure.

Paul conceived of his remaining *in the flesh* as a further opportunity to witness, to work, to woo, and to win other trophies for his dear Lord. He is sure there will be some *fruit* of his work. Nothing less than that hope could hold him for a moment. Were it not for the joy of telling the story and constraining men to accept Christ, he would much prefer striking his tent, breaking camp, loosing the moorings, and leaving for that better country at once. He really has a great longing to leave for home (2 Cor. 5:1-8). This is one of the most poignantly beautiful of all Paul's lines.

Would that all of us could subscribe to the idea that the purpose of our lives is winning souls. What would such an idea do to the millions of older Christians who are lingering on here? It would certainly lighten the way and take all the fear out of "that dark valley." It would set us on the main track and make us aware of the real reason for living. We might see that life is worth living. The oldest Christian among us, if imbued with Paul's passion for Christ, could win lost souls by the scores.

Paul concludes that the one reason for him to remain *in the flesh* is the very definite need he feels to continue with the churches, the Christians, and the work. He believes that they need him. His obligation to them looms larger and heavier. He must postpone the joys of being with Christ in order that more souls may be won and more Christians taught the doctrines of Christ. He will live out his remaining days proving the full meaning of his pronouncement *to me to live is Christ*.

HEAVENLY CITIZENSHIP (27–30)

Paul assures his readers that he plans to live out the rest of his earthly life as a citizen of "the colony of heaven" should live it; he would live a life that is *worthy of the gospel*. Our word "conversation" used to carry more of this idea than it does at present. The Greek word has to do with much more than the speaking of words; it includes the thoughts, the words, and the deeds of each person. The things he thinks, the words he speaks, and the deeds of his hands are to be *worthy of the gospel*. He is constantly in the presence of the Holy Spirit, who knows each thought, hears each word, and sees each deed. All of life must be lived according to the spiritual standard set by our Lord and Saviour. The whole of human life is sweetened and made beautiful by the teachings of Christ. There will be a big difference in the way you live if you are always aware of His blessed presence. Try it.

Stand fast (27): Moral steadfastness marks the citizen who recognizes Christ's presence. He finds new stamina, new staying qualities, new courage, new strength with which to carry on. Daniel is a good example of such firm power in the inner man. The martyrs stood resolutely even in the moment of death. Paul would have his good friends stand as powerfully in life.

With one mind striving together (27): Paul cannot get away from the idea of intense struggle and ceaseless activity in presenting the gospel. He wants a shoulder-to-shoulder onslaught against the devil and all his army; he urges a united effort—spirited, vigorous, ceaseless, and powerful. Every ounce of his strength is thrown into the struggle. The Philippians, too, are to throw all their resources and energies into the contest. Nothing short of complete commitment will do. What would happen in your church if this ideal could be reached? Is there good reason to fail? Paul speaks as pleadingly to us as to the Philippians. Lost souls, by the thousands, wait for such concerted effort. The Holy Spirit begs us to let Him work through us. What is your response?

In nothing terrified (28): Paul says, "Never be scared, like a frightened horse, in the face of opposition." He wants courage to be in evidence every day. These people in Philippi represent the Lord Jesus. They possess eternal life. They have the continual presence of the Holy Spirit. They have deep convictions that are worth dying for. Why should they shy like a scared colt? Why should their testimonies be weakened by timidity and fear?

It is given . . . believe . . . suffer . . . conflict (29–30): Paul would have his friends take account of the fact that when each Christian is given the privilege of personal faith in Christ, he is also given the privilege of suffering as a fully dedicated follower. Even martyrdom is a special gift if it makes the gospel effective.

Suffering is a gift from the divine hand. By means of it the character is built, sweetened, purified, and made beautiful. Because of it others are taught the finer strands of Christian faith and character. Souls are challenged to come to Christ for salvation and life commitment. Life is a continuing struggle. It is a conflict, a wrestling bout with the forces of the devil. It is never easy. Life was not easy for Paul in the prison at Philippi; it was not easy during his harrowing experiences in Rome. God never intended that life should be lived without terrific struggle.

SUMMARY

Paul has called you to put your trembling hand in the powerful hand of the Lord Jesus. As a result of that full dedication, you may expect a *conflict* (29–30) that will demand complete participation in the warfare with the devil, in the never-ending wrestle with the powers of the evil one. You may expect to live a *gospel-worthy life* (27). Thoughts, words, deeds, and attitudes will all be seen in the light of the presence of the Master. The Holy Spirit is present night and day. Every thought, every word is known. You may expect unusual *courage* (28) in every encounter with the devil and in every contact with those who need salvation. You may count on power to overcome and power to *drive out fears* (28). The conquest of fear is a certainty. You may expect a beautiful *steadfastness* (27) that reveals strands of character seldom found among human beings. You may know unusual powers of mind, body, and spirit. You can certainly expect a *consecration* (21) that will make you radiant.

Paul gives an insight into his own heart and triumphantly affirms, *For to me to live is Christ!* That is living! That can happen to you.

May this chapter grip your mind, heart, and soul. May

you determine that Christ shall be magnified in your body and that all life through you will seek to make these glowing truths come alive. Remember the Holy Spirit stands ready to see you through every moment of the journey. *For to me to live is Christ.*

Ephesians III

That the Gentiles should be fellowheirs, and of the same body, and partakers of his promise in Christ by the gospel: whereof I was made a minister. . . . Unto me, who am less than the least of all saints, is this grace given, that I should preach among the Gentiles the unsearchable riches of Christ; and to make all men see what is the fellowship of the mystery, which from the beginning of the world hath been hid in God. . . .

For this cause I bow my knees unto the Father of our Lord Jesus Christ . . . that he would grant you, according to the riches of his glory, to be strengthened with might by his Spirit in the inner man; that Christ may dwell in your hearts by faith; that ye, being rooted and grounded in love, may be able to comprehend with all saints what is the breadth, and length, and depth, and height; and to know the love of Christ, which passeth knowledge, that ye might be filled with all the fulness of God.

Now unto him that is able to do exceeding abundantly above all that we ask or think, according to the power that worketh in us, unto him be glory in the church by Christ Jesus throughout all ages, world without end. Amen.

XIII. Paul's Mighty Prayer

_____*Ephesians III*

T HE CHALLENGE of the second chapter of Paul's letter to the Ephesian Christians still rings in our ears and stirs our hearts. The apostle had reached great heights in telling of the living sanctuary. This structure was made up of Jews and Gentiles who had been redeemed by the blood of Christ, saved by the grace of God, filled with the power of the Holy Spirit, and built into the very structure of God's holy temple that glory might come to the divine Name continually. In a long digression Paul interpreted *the mystery of Christ* and the part that he plays in the proclamation of that mystery. He told of his commission and the revelation that came to him concerning the sacred secret that had waited so long before coming to men's hearts. Then he began to pray that these Christians might fulfil their calling and carry out the will of the Redeemer.

PREPARATION FOR THE PRAYER (2–13)

The prisoner of Jesus Christ (1): Since his experience on the Damascus road Paul had been unusually conscious of the fact that he belonged to the Lord. "Whether we live or die,

195

we belong to the Lord," he had said (Rom. 14:8). He spoke of himself as apostle, bondslave, prisoner. He could not get away from the powerful "tap on the shoulder" that had arrested him and made him a literal prisoner of Christ. For four years he had been under the strong hand of the Roman officials who had used chains to impress him with the fact of his bondage. During those years he was always aware that it was because of his love for his Saviour that his real "imprisonment" came.

In behalf of you (1): He reminded the Gentiles that he was in prison because of his vigorous and stubborn insistence that the gospel must include men of all races, languages, and colors. The Jews could not allow such heresy, and Paul was thrown into prison. He was literally a *prisoner of Jesus Christ* in behalf of those to whom he wrote. His stripes, his chains, and his sufferings were endured because he dared fulfil Christ's commission to go to them with the gospel.

The mystery of Christ (3): We have come to think of a mystery as something unintelligible or perplexing. In Paul's writings it is a deep truth revealed or communicated to a person who is in touch with God. The mystery Paul spoke of was perfectly simple and apparent after God revealed it to him. It had been God's secret, but it became the precious possession of the one to whom God gave it. For Paul it was the simple fact that God's full welcome was freely waiting for Gentile as well as Jew, that all races are equal in God's love and in His plan. This had been God's "secret" through the ages, as He waited for a redeemed family through whom He might proclaim this glorious truth.

The stewardship of grace (2): God's grace has always abounded. It has been plenteous. It has constituted a full reservoir. Always it has been available to all. Paul tells us that the special responsibility of taking that grace to the

Gentiles had been entrusted to him. His was a sublime privilege, but it carried with it a burdensome responsibility. The apostle had a divinely given trust that must command the best that he could give as long as life lasted. Needy hearts all over the world waited for his message.

By revelation (3): That special commission to preach the gospel to the Gentiles had been given to Paul when he became a Christian. His special revelation from God Himself came both at that time and in a fuller measure during his prolonged stay in Arabia (Gal. 1:12, 17). Visions and special revelations later brought additional messages from the divine throne. Someone has said, "Paul went into Arabia with Moses and the prophets in his knapsack and returned to Damascus with the Romans and the Ephesians in his mouth and in his heart." The marvelous teachings put forth by the great apostle came through a sublime revelation. He was in tune with God, and the time was ripe for the revelation of God's great secret. What could be more natural than the giving of that glorious "mystery" through Paul?

Fellow heirs (6) : As a result of their being *in Christ,* the Gentiles became fellow heirs, fellow members, fellow partakers. Grace—the amazing grace of God—made their salvation possible. The atoning death of the Lord Jesus purchased their redemption. A simple act of faith made salvation complete. God's secret has been revealed.

Practically all the commentators interpret this passage as the words themselves would indicate: *fellow heirs*—children of God, brethren of Christ, actual heirs of the Father's bounty; fellow members *of the same body*—each believer having equality in the kingdom; fellow partakers of *his promise*—each believer eligible for every fulfilment of all the prophecies and promises. Dr. W. O. Carver states: " 'The Gentiles are jointly (with Jews) the inheritance' of God in the human race; 'are (along with the Jews) within the Body' of Christ which is being created and grown in the Christian movement; 'and are equal sharers in the promise (which is offered and to be realized) in Christ Jesus,' the one mediator between God and all men." [1] In Dr. Carver's understanding, the Gentiles are not pictured as *joint-heirs* but as a *joint-inheritance*. Paul was under deep conviction that such a divine secret demanded urgent preaching of the message to all the people of all the earth. How do we explain our lack of zeal and urgency in the light of a passage like this? All men must be given the gospel message because only in Christ can these blessings come to men. Surely we will tell them!

I was made a minister (7): The plan of God was so big, the news was so startling, the need was so great, the salvation was so wonderful, the terms were so simple, and the privileges so satisfying that we are not surprised to hear Paul say that he "was made a minister." The heavy hand of God reached out and pulled him in. The commission of God found him, and a burden was laid on him. The divine secret was entrusted to him. Immortal souls, out in the great beyond, were dependent on his coming to them. *The working of His power* made Paul a minister. His was a divinely ordered call, a divinely given commission. It made a profound impression on him. God had convinced him that the ultimate success of the plan rested, in a large measure, upon his shoulders.

That I should preach (8): Paul has used the word "minister." He now uses the word "preach." He is to interpret the will and word of God to men groping in tragic darkness. He is to proclaim life-changing good news to lost men and "throw light on" the stewardship of the deepest purpose of God.

---

[1] *The Glory of God in the Christian Calling* (Nashville: Broadman Press, 1949), p. 130.

Suddenly he realizes how pitifully inadequate he is, how totally unworthy he is, how pathetically out of place it will be for one who has been the persecutor of the church to be God's messenger to proclaim the truth. In true humility he faces the inventory and presents himself to his Father as a sinner saved by grace. He will do the Master's bidding.

The unsearchable riches of Christ (8): The word *unsearchable* (cf. Rom. 11:33) means literally "that which cannot be traced out or comprehended." The riches of Christ are so rich, so deep, so untrackable, that it is beyond our power to know and grasp and understand them fully. Thanks be to God that there are so many beautiful and useful treasures that are available and at hand. Fortunate indeed is the man to whom God has entrusted the signal honor of revealing these riches. Happy is the man who is privileged to preach God's word! It is given to him to illuminate all men. He will be privileged to throw a bright light on truths that have been in the shadow, to show God's love so that men may see and understand and believe. He is to lead in the worldwide distribution of the news and the blessings of the full gospel. God's great secret must be brought to every ear. His prescription for life must be given to every soul. Paul was thrilled to realize that he had been chosen to lead in this task. He would be dedicated to the task.

Might be made known by the church (10): The glorious work of the kingdom of God is not to be confined to the apostle. It is also to be given to the church with the command that these wondrous truths be made known to all the people of the earth. These new creatures in Christ, who had experienced the miracle of salvation, are to witness to all other needy ones with enthusiasm and flaming zeal until all shall know the saving power available through the vicarious suffering of the Son of God. The work of the church is not an afterthought of God. It is all within the eternal plan of God. His Son had been set apart from the foundation of the world as the Lamb of God who should take away the sin of the world. His part was worked out in His atoning death. The proclamation of the good news, the witnessing to the saving power, and the carrying of the secret of God to all people would be the particular work of His church. They were entrusted with the "much-variegated" wisdom of God. All of the intricate depths of God's dealing with sin, pardon, and salvation were included in the precious treasure they were to carry to needy men. Every problem and every difficulty had been met by the Redeemer in His act of expiation. The members of the church were free to present the heavenly message to all who were willing to hear.

Powers in heavenly places (3:10): Are the angels interested in the gospel and its power to save? Are they to be considered in the proclamation of the good news of salvation? Peter wrote that these were "things angels covet to look upon" (1 Pet. 1:12). The amazing grace of God is unusually interesting in its working. Multitudes are drawn to watch its working in human hearts. Even the heavenly hosts are concerned and curious to learn of the manifold grace of God as it is manifested in the redemption of immortal souls. Paul knew that the church of the living Christ is to be an object of wonder and amazement to heavenly beings. In the work of the church these beings are to see and understand the wisdom of God.

The amazing miracle of God's grace will always be an object of wonder to men and angels. This idea presents a new challenge to us as we link ourselves with Paul and the other saints of all the earth and all the ages in revealing the wisdom of God. May God give us unusual power to succeed in that which lies deepest in the plan and purpose of

Christ. We can astonish the angels with a new and thrilling display of the power of God as it works miracles of grace in human hearts.

G. G. Findlay, in the *Expositor's Bible,* says:

The magnitude and completeness of this plan is indicated in the fact that it embraces in its purview *the angelic powers and their enlightenment.* . . . Christ's service is the high school of wisdom for the universe. . . . The revelations of the latter days—the incarnation, the cross, the publication of the gospel, the outpouring of the Spirit—were full of surprises to the heavenly watchers. . . . It is not from the abstract scheme of salvation, from the theory or the theology of the Church that they get this education, but through the living Church herself.[1]

It is exhilarating to know that by proclaiming and extending the gospel we help the universe know God.

Boldness . . . access . . . confidence (12): Paul describes for us the unusual privileges we can enjoy as we participate in the holy calling of Christ Jesus. *Boldness* here has to do with unlimited freedom of speech. It is the boldness of free and intimate intercourse in God's presence. In Hebrews 4:14–16 we are assured that we can approach the throne of God unafraid and unabashed through Jesus our great High Priest. We come with free utterance to the throne of grace to speak a child's every thought and wish.

That holy *boldness* may apply in the realm of preaching —the proclamation of the gospel message to people of all nations and languages. Paul realizes that he is God's steward of the mystery of grace. He knows that he is working in accordance with God's plan of the ages. He is thrilled by the eyes of the heavenly watchers who stand ready to see and

---

[1] *The Epistle to the Ephesians* (New York: Hodder & Stroughton, n.d.), pp. 169, 172–73.

know the infinite reaches of God's grace. He is, therefore, emboldened to preach without fear the full gospel in every ear that can be reached. We have full boldness to say, either to God or to men, all that is in our hearts. Being a member of God's family through faith in Christ makes the difference. Through experience Paul had found that he could be bold. He knew fully the rare privilege that was his.

Access means literally "introduction." Paul reminds himself that he owes his intimate relationship at the throne and his powerful entrance into the hearts of men to the introduction given by the Lord Jesus. This access was first secured by the Redeemer's work, and it is kept alive by the constant presence of the living Christ who "ever liveth to make intercession for us" (Heb. 7:25). Paul knows that the presence of the Holy Spirit surrounds and empowers and animates him in every moment of his ministry. Because of the Spirit's work, the servant of God is free, in praying or in preaching, to enter the secret place with God or to enter the hearts of men with the burning message of the gospel.

Confidence is a powerful bit of equipment for one who would walk with God or speak to men. It is the special boon of those who are in Christ and comes *through faith* in Him. That choice relationship enjoyed by the apostle makes possible a buoyant, powerful approach to his significant work. He has won the victory even before he speaks a word. Faith in Christ has opened the door and prepared the way and written the verdict beforehand. The Holy Spirit prepares the speaker, moves the heart of the hearer, brings on conviction and encouragement, walks with the believer to the place of commitment, and then performs the miracle of salvation. Paul assures the Gentile Christians at Ephesus that these privileges are to be theirs, that these victories can be accomplished in them. This *boldness,* this *introduction,* this *confidence* can be their treasures and the victories that follow can give a moving demonstration of the grace of God to the people of the earth and to the heavenly watchers.

Paul has written of the missionary task, the true missionary spirit, and the privilege of sharing Christ's redemption with others. He knows the all-sufficient grace of God and the unlimited power of God to animate and empower the weakest disciple to win others to our Lord and Saviour. Thanks be unto God who has committed to us, also, the task of telling the good news to the waiting millions.

THE PRAYER (14–19)

After writing of the great work of the church and of his part in that task, Paul remembered the church to which he was writing. As he remembered, he was moved to pray for that church, expressing himself in petitions of sweep and elevation. That prayer is one of the mountain peaks of praying recorded in the Bible. The language is high and exalted, the spirit deep and profound. The petitions are personal and individual even as they reach in wonderful range to all the members of God's redeemed family.

It is for the church that Paul is concerned. He wants each individual to be so strong, so virile, so spiritual, and so lovable that Christ may have a place in which He may dwell, a sphere in which He may work, an instrument through which the Holy Spirit may win His mightiest victories. Paul wants the church to be so clean and spiritual and lovable that it may be filled to the entire fulness of God's redeeming purpose. How fervently he prays for the church! How ardent are his hopes for her triumphant progress toward the fullest realization of Christ's dreams for her!

I bend my knees (14): In his earlier prayer (1:16) Paul had said, "I cease not to make mention of you in my prayers." It was unusual to bow in prayer, but this was an unusual moment in Paul's experience. He was expressing unusual earnestness, reverence, and humility. It was an occasion that called for the fullest prostration of himself before the eternal Father. Not only were Paul's knees bent but his entire body fell to the ground before God, his posture marking deep reverence (cf. Phil. 2:10). He recognized the eternal God as the Father of every person who had come into the church through faith in Christ. God is the Father of all mankind in the sense that He is the Creator of all, but He becomes the spiritual Father only as the individual, by the new birth, becomes a new creature in Christ. Paul did not discover the true fatherhood of God until he came to know Jesus Christ as his Saviour. To this Father he makes three petitions.

According to the riches of his glory (16): How could the imagination take in all the reaches of this concept? Paul was in the heights and thought in terms of the sublime and the measureless resources of the eternal God. Let us bear in mind this limitless supply when we follow him in his three petitions.

Strengthened with power by his Spirit (16): Paul prays that the church may be made the fit dwelling place for Christ. Each individual must be an integral part of that holy body in order to make it an acceptable residence for Christ. He must dwell in His church to carry on His work of redemption, restoration, and sanctification. Spiritual strength must be available in each unit. Men of faith must be prepared in heart, mind, and will.

The Holy Spirit provides the power; it is through His quickening ministry that the heart is able to contain and appropriate that power. As He moves freely within, that power is communicated and made available for Christ as He uses the church for world conquest. You may be a small one in the kingdom, but you are tremendously important in Christ's plan. You may mar His plan by your failure or by your refusal to be used in the church. Paul is praying for you.

In the inner man (16): The place of real need is the inner man. Christ's work depends upon the right sort of hearts in the members of His church. Outward show or profession is worthless if the heart is wrong. "Keep thy heart with all diligence; for out of it are the issues of life" (Prov. 4:23). The inward man is our total inner nature—the will, the emotions, the intellect. In the writings of Paul we see the power of God concentrated in the inner life of the believer. Moral strengthening, spiritual understanding, and growth in knowledge are recognized as the supreme needs of those who would exhibit the love of Christ in the world. Soul enrichment is the supreme need of the believer. (Cf. 2 Cor. 4:16; Rom. 7:22.)

Inner strengthening will make possible power for a worthy walk before God. The Holy Spirit provides power for the warfare (cf. 1 Cor. 10:13). It is through His work that there is power for witnessing (cf. Acts 1:8; 4:33). The Holy Spirit also provides power for weaknesses (cf. 2 Cor. 12:7–10; 1 Cor. 4:7; Phil. 4:13). Power is plentifully provided. How marvelous is the provision made possible for those who are in Christ! It is the Father's wish that each of His redeemed children shall accept and be blessed by the power which He provides. The Holy Spirit seeks to find an individual through whom the full power of God may find expression. Do you know any good reason why you should refuse Him? He delights to empower one who will be successful in the task of witnessing to the saving power of Christ's atonement.

That Christ may dwell in your hearts by faith (17): Can

we become fit residences for Christ? Paul prays that we may become such places. Christ has asked for this privilege. He has sent the Holy Spirit to make our hearts ready. Only our own stubborn selfishness can keep Him out, and we will be the poorer if we refuse Him. He will recognize our ingratitude and our unwillingness to help set forward the cause. Others will go without the gospel if we refuse to let Him in. Each passing year will record a gradual deepening of spiritual affection, a richer spiritual temperature, and a fuller harvest of fruit for our Lord. He will purify the affections, enlighten the understanding, and control the will.

Paul's theme has been *in Christ*. He turns now to the other side and demands *Christ in you* (cf. Col. 1:27). Father, Son, and Holy Spirit bring to the humble believer the rich blessings so sorely needed if he is to assume his responsibility in making up the true church of our Lord and Saviour.

Rooted and grounded in love (17): A tree is firmly rooted, and a building is solidly set on a secure foundation. The saints are thought of as "trees" of the Lord set deep in the rich soil of love and as "prepared stones" built securely upon an enduring foundation. In both figures there is a challenge to the highest devotion to our Lord. He has always exhibited the richer qualities of love in His life and in His teachings. When Christ is continually present in your life, you are securely settled and deeply founded in the very essence of love. It is an abiding principle of your life.

Strong to comprehend (18): Only together in co-operation and under full stimulation can we hope to explore the depths of this magnificent love. Together, Spirit-led men can make their way up the precipitous heights until many of the hitherto undiscovered glories can be caught, enjoyed, and appropriated. It is rare revelation that Paul is giving. Only saints that are adventurous because they are strangely assured of their footing can hope to climb the different ascents. How thrilling the challenge! Remember the Holy Spirit is near *to lead you into all truth.* Undiscovered realms of truth loom before us as we walk with Him.

Breadth . . . length . . . depth . . . height (18): How can you deal with this sublime illustration of the vast reaches of the love of God? That love is "broad," extending to all people on the face of the earth. It is "long," reaching through all time backward and forward, from before the foundations of the earth to the endless ages of eternity. It is "high," to the very throne room of the eternal God. It is "deep," to the lowest condition of human need. Instead of planning specific measurements, Paul pictured a love that is beyond all estimate and description. It truly *passes all knowledge.* You and I must seek diligently the *breadth* and *length* and *depth* and *height* of God's matchless love.

Know the love of Christ (19): The apostle prayed that his friends might come to see the love of God, as it was expressed through Christ, as real, as colorful, as full and abounding, as life-changing, and as His own most characteristic portrait for men to see. The word "know" (an aorist verb) pictures a new and decisive knowledge of a spiritual kind. It can come only as the individual, in deep love for Christ, comes to know Him and understand His love and His nature. It is achieved only in this unique relationship of full commitment of oneself to Christ. Are you willing to know the love of Christ? There will always be unexplored depths to lure you on to a fuller understanding'. The Holy Spirit is with you to help you in your search.

The fulness of God (19): The prayer comes to its grand climax in this petition that the church may come to demonstrate the full purpose of God in human history. The Father must see the members come up to the holy ideal so completely that they will give a full demonstration of His intent in creation, in providence, and in redemption. Everything that God hoped, planned, and projected in His eternal purpose must be realized in the church. He has put His all into the church. Everything Christians have and are must be poured into the effort to produce a result that will be pleasing to the eyes of the holy God. His ideal must be realized. Dr. W. O. Carver said: "Only as the whole Body of Christ can the redeemed be filled 'up to all the fulness of God.' That is the goal. Here in this total, summary prayer are the processes and the stages in the complete significance of the Christ of God in history." [2]

We can become increasingly like our Lord and Saviour who exhibited the graces and qualities that make up *the fulness of God* (cf. Col. 1:9; Rom. 15:13; Col. 2:9; 2 Pet. 1:4). Paul puts before us an impossible goal, but one that will challenge us step by step, day by day until we shall be *like Him*. Study Paul's picture in 2 Cor. 3:18: "We all, with unveiled face, beholding as in a mirror the glory of the Lord, are transformed into the same image from glory to glory." In another beautiful promise we read, "We shall be like him; for we shall see him as he is" (1 John 3:2).

THE DOXOLOGY (3:20–21)

The lofty prayer with its bold petitions is followed by a beautiful hymn of praise to the all-powerful God who is able to answer Paul's great prayer. Paul had begged for moral excellence, spiritual growth, and power in preaching that seemed to be beyond the range of possibility. In this magnificent burst of praise he assures all men that they are dealing with the one great Answerer who is able to give even

---

[2] Carver, *op. cit.*, p. 140.

more than anyone of them could ever ask. There is no limit to His power. He can reach back into His limitless reservoir of treasures and supply the answer. His power is already working within us. It is constant. It will never cease. (Cf. Col. 1:29; 1 Thess. 3:10.)

Glory is given to the Father. All the praise and thanksgiving and glory that can be heaped up is sent to the throne room above. That praise is to be continuous and eternal, constantly going up to Him.

> Praise God, from whom all blessings flow;
> Praise Him, all creatures here below;
> Praise Him above, ye heav'nly host;
> Praise Father, Son, and Holy Ghost.
>
> THOMAS KEN